WRITING AND SELLING
CHILDREN'S BOOKS
IN THE CHRISTIAN MARKET

WRITING AND SELLING CHILDREN'S BOOKS IN THE CHRISTIAN MARKET

FROM BOARD BOOK TO YA

CYLE YOUNG &
MICHELLE MEDLOCK ADAMS

Birmingham, Alabama

New Hope Publishers
100 Missionary Ridge
Birmingham, AL 35242
An imprint of Iron Stream Media
NewHopePublishers.com
IronStreamMedia.com

© 2020 by Cyle Young and Michelle Medlock Adams
All rights reserved. First printing 2020
Printed in the United States of America.

No part of this publication may be reproduced, stored in a retrieval system, or transmitted in any form or by any means—electronic, mechanical, photocopying, recording, or otherwise—without the prior written permission of the publisher.

Library of Congress Control Number: 2020949039

All Scripture quotations, unless otherwise indicated, are taken from The Holy Bible, English Standard Version, copyright © 2001 by Crossway Bibles, a division of Good News Publishers. Used by permission. All rights reserved.

Scripture quotations marked (NIV) are taken from the Holy Bible, New International Version®, NIV®. Copyright © 1973, 1978, 1984, 2011 by Biblica, Inc.™ Used by permission of Zondervan. All rights reserved worldwide. www.zondervan.com The "NIV" and "New International Version" are trademarks registered in the United States Patent and Trademark Office by Biblica, Inc.™

ISBN-13: 978-1-56309-407-1
E-book ISBN: 978-1-56309-408-8

1 2 3 4 5—24 23 22 21 20

Dedication

From "Gigi" Michelle: For Bear, Bo-Riley, Wren, and Walter "Boone" who have given me an even greater desire to share the goodness of God through story …

From Cyle: To my wonderful wife, Patty, and amazing children, Carver, Cyleigh-Anne, and Carrick. Thanks for putting up with all the countless hours writing and agenting. You all are the best!

Contents

Acknowledgments xiii

Foreword xv
    Dandi Daley Mackall

Introduction xvii
    Cyle Young

Section 1: Writing Children's Books 1

A Writer's Journey: Victoria Duerstock 1

1 Writing Christian Children's Books—It's a Calling 3
    Michelle Medlock Adams

2 What Makes a Great "High-Concept" Idea? 7
    Cyle Young

3 Writing Books that Make a Difference 13
    Michelle Medlock Adams

Author Nuggets of Wisdom: Janet Surette 17

4 The Top Three Misconceptions for Writing in the
    Christian Children's Book Market 19
    Michelle Medlock Adams

An Editor's Journey: Peggy Schaefer 23

5 The Differences between Age Groups 25
    Cyle Young

6 Writing and Publishing a Series 31
    Ashley Jones

7 Storytelling for Children 37
    Steven James

8 Know Your Audience 41
    Rachel Pellegrino

9 Injecting a Dose of Humor into Your Children's Book 47
    Doug Peterson

Author Nuggets of Wisdom: Melody Delgado 52

10 Breathe New Life into an Old Concept 53
    Michelle Medlock Adams

11 Writing Strong Characters 57
    Nancy I. Sanders

12 Writing Back Matter that Matters 61
    Nancy I. Sanders

13 Writing for the Educational Market 67
    Wendy Hinote Lanier

An Editor's Journey: Deb Haggerty 72

Section 2: Young Children's Books—Board Book to Picture Book 73

A Writer's Journey: Megan Alms 73

14 Board Books 75
    Jill Roman Lord

15 Thinking in Pictures and Writing Visually 79
    P. K. Hallinan

16 Picture Book Plots 83
    Shannon Anderson

17 Rhythm, Rhyme, and Repetition: Mastering the
Skill of Writing in Verse 87
Crystal Bowman

18 Crafting Holiday Books that Sell 93
Michelle Medlock Adams

An Editor's Journey: Steve Bootsma 98

19 Interactive Books 99
Robin Currie

Section 3: Older Children's Books—Early Readers to YA 103

A Writer's Journey: Hope Bolinger 103

20 Devotions 105
Michelle Medlock Adams

21 Biographies 111
Nancy Lohr

22 The World of Chapter Books 115
Dandi Daley Mackall

23 Three Keys to Writing Biblical Truth for Children 119
Christopher Maselli

Author Nuggets of Wisdom: Amy Houts 123

24 Writing for Middle Grade 125
Tim Shoemaker

25 Writing Craft Books 131
Karen Whiting

26 Writing Nonfiction for YA 137
Bethany Jett

An Editor's Journey: Karissa Taylor 140

27 Writing YA that Sells in the Christian Market 143
Caroline George

28 Writing YA Fiction: What Teens Really Want to
Hear and What They Don't 149
Tessa Hall

Author Nuggets of Wisdom: Alyssa Roat 153

Section 4: Selling Children's Books 155

A Writer's Journey: Debbie Spence 155

29 Platform 157
Cyle Young

Author Nuggets of Wisdom: Lori Z. Scott 160

30 Query with Confidence 163
Michelle Medlock Adams

31 Proposals 171
Cyle Young

Author Nuggets of Wisdom: Jennifer Froelich 176

32 Writing and Selling to Christian Magazines 179
Lori Z. Scott

Author Nuggets of Wisdom: Amanda Flinn 183

33 Author Visits 185
Shannon Anderson

34 Networking 191
Cyle Young

35 Six Tips to Make Your Book Signing Successful 193
Michelle Medlock Adams

Author Nuggets of Wisdom: Art Ginolfi 197

36 Winning Strategies to Get Your Books in the Hands of Young Readers 199
Mary Morgan

37 Self-Publishing Your Books 203
Catherine Jones Payne

38 The Difference between the Markets: Christian to General 209
Cyle Young

39 Work for Hire 215
Tracie Heskett

An Editor's Journey: Catherine DeVries 220

Section 5: Extra Advice 223

A Writer's Journey: Caroline George 223

40 Motivation and Reaction 225
Bryan Davis

Author Nuggets of Wisdom: Catherine Jones Payne 231

41 Find the Heart of Your Story 233
Michelle Medlock Adams

42 Contests 237
Cyle Young

43 Contracts 241
Cyle Young

44 Agents in the Christian Market 245
Cyle Young

45 Ghostwriting and Adapting Books 247
Tama Fortner

46 The Research Trail 253
Wendy Hinote Lanier

47 Diversity 257
    Edwina Perkins

Conclusion 261
    Cyle Young

Contributor Biographies 263

Acknowledgments

From Michelle: First off, I want to thank God for allowing me to write for His precious children. It's one of the greatest privileges of my life. Also, I want to thank my wonderful husband, Jeff. You're the best husband, Daddy, Pops, and fishing partner in the world. I am so grateful for your constant support and unconditional love. I also want to thank Abby and Ally, my amazing daughters, who have inspired most of my children's stories. I love both of you "Bigger than the sky."

Thanks also to my amazing agent Cyle Young for believing in me, encouraging me, selling my books, counseling me when I need it, and for being one of my closest friends. I am so blessed that I get to "do life" with you and Patty, Bethany and Justin, Del and Angie, Cody and Bethany, Andy and Crystal, Victoria Duerstock, Ashley Jones, and the rest of our little literary family. Love you all!

And, to the children's authors who have inspired me, taught me, and cheered me on, I say a big thank you. Dandi Daley Mackall, Crystal Bowman, Pk Hallinan, Christopher Maselli (and Gena too!), Steven James, Nancy Sanders, Wendy Hinote Lanier (and the rest of the NF Ninjas!!), Karen Whiting, and so many others—thank you for being so excellent and so willing to share your knowledge. To my longtime editors and dear friends—the Peggys—Peggy Kuethe and Peggy Schaefer—I say, "Thank you for taking a chance on me and continuing to believe in my writing.

You're amazing editors and even better friends. Love you both!"

And, to Karissa Taylor, Ramona Richards, Pat Pingry, Melinda Rathjen, Barbara Scott, Gwen Ellis, Carol Layton and Nancy Lohr—thank you for making me a better children's writer. You've all made a difference in my life.

From Cyle: Thank you to my coauthor and friend, Michelle Medlock Adams. I am so thankful to have been mentored by you in children's writing. Your friendship and investment in me helped shape me into the author and agent that I am, and I continue to strive to do the same for my clients and other authors. I also want to thank all my author friends and clients who have trusted me to assist them in their careers and writing journeys. We are all in this together.

To each of the amazing and best-selling authors who shared their insights in one of the chapters contained within this book. Thank you! Michelle and I chose you because we value your passion for this industry and the vibrancy with which you write and share Christ.

To John Herring, Ramona Richards, and Iron Stream Media, we heartily thank you for believing in us and believing in this book. We are excited to help equip other generations of writers to share the light of Christ, one manuscript at a time.

Foreword
Dandi Daley Mackall

You are a writer, whether you've not yet published a single word, or you've published hundreds of books. Most people hate to write, but you fight for time to do just that. You enjoy writing enough that you've decided to read this book about writing for children. And the title alone should validate your decision, especially if your focus is both writing and selling in the Christian market.

As a Christian writer, your writing can also be your ministry. When I ended my time as a missionary behind the Iron Curtain (during the Soviet Union's communist control of Eastern Europe), I felt as if I were ending my ministry. But I'd written my first book while in Poland, an adult nonfiction I had to write by hand, snuggled under a pile of blankets to keep from freezing. When I returned to the United States, I kept writing, eventually, after I had kids, focusing on children's books. I added age groups as they grew older: a baby book, board books, picture books, early readers, chapter books, middle-grade, young adult (YA). God had given me another ministry, writing.

First Thessalonians 4:1 says: "Finally then, brethren, we request and exhort you in the Lord Jesus, that as you received from us instruction as to how you ought to walk and please God (just as you actually do walk), that you excel still more."

To help equip you to excel still more, the editors of this book have gathered successful children's authors and industry specialists to share practical insights and advice for writing every genre, for every age group. They share their experiences and hard-earned knowledge on breaking into Christian markets, going to the next level, marketing, building a platform to sell your manuscripts and your books. Plus, you'll find the latest publishing advice from expert editors of major Christian publishing houses.

We pray you will glean everything you need from these pages, and then go and write your heart out!

At the Last Supper, after Jesus washed His disciples' feet, He told them, "Now that you know these things, you will be blessed if you do them" (John 13:17).

Introduction
Cyle Young

When I started out as a literary agent, I could've never imagined that I would have contracted three hundred works on behalf of my authors and illustrators. But just under four years later, I crossed that threshold when we contracted a two-book fiction deal with Focus on the Family. The beginning of my literary agent journey has been a whirlwind of conferences, contracts, and book releases. How did so much success happen in such a short amount of time?

- Timing?
- Providence?
- Hard work?

I'll be honest, I never intended to be a full-time literary agent essentially, but when God opens doors, and you keep stepping through, you'll always find yourself at the center of His will. As an author, I had a couple of bad agent experiences. I was represented by agents who unfortunately took me on as a client in the middle of life change and crisis. One day, I made the mistake of telling another agent of my frustration. I shared that I was sure I could do better for my clients if I ever became an agent. After sharing my version of a "95 Theses" with the agent, I was offered the opportunity to join their team, and a few days later, I accepted.

My plan was simple. I'd noticed that no agent in the Christian market focused on representing children's authors. Some agents represented a couple of children's authors, but no one had built an entire client roster of them. I knew if I could attract the most talented authors, I could sell their books to attract more clients—and that's exactly the business model I used to build a list of over 150 authors and illustrators. I currently represent all genres and markets, but I "cut my teeth" in the Christian children's market. I have a huge passion for children's literature, and I love to see new works created and published for children.

My first few clients were awesome children's book authors who already had some success: Jill Roman Lord and Robin Currie trusted me with their books. We were able to get them book contracts, and shortly after, I was approached by a children's author I'd always hoped to work with—Michelle Medlock Adams. Michelle was my instructor and mentor when I first started attending writer's conferences. She literally writes books in her mind while she's brushing her teeth. She leaks children's books.

Partnering together, we quickly sold twelve books in one year. Two years later, during the Selah Awards—the biggest awards ceremony for Christian children's book authors—all four of the finalists were my authors. Jill Roman Lord had two books in the finals, and Robin Currie and Michelle Medlock Adams both had one. Three of the four titles received perfect scores, and Jill's book, *That Grand Christmas Day,* not only won the category, she also took most prestigious prize—the overall book of the year award. Her book beat out over one hundred other finalists.

I tell you this not to brag or boast, but to encourage you that the information included in this book is birthed

Introduction

out of a passion for children's books, from board books to YA. Michelle and I share years of combined industry experience to help you succeed. Michelle publishes in multiple genres and age categories, and she's won numerous awards in all of them. She's published almost one hundred titles in her career, selling close to four million copies, and she's not slowing down. I have followed Michelle's lead, and I also write in multiple genres and age categories. As an agent, I have sold books in every genre and age category in the Christian market. We write this book from our personal experiences with the hope that we can impart insights and wisdom to you to help you achieve your publishing goals.

Some of our favorite authors have contributed to this book to help you on your writing journey. From seasoned pros to emerging children's book authors, these contributors have shared their expert advice and insider tips, and you get to benefit from their wisdom in the following pages. Who knows? Maybe you'll be one of our featured authors when we write another volume of this resource in future years. Your first or next book contract might be in the works right now. It could happen, and when it does, we want to celebrate your publishing success with you. Please let Michelle and me know when that day comes, and we will be the first to congratulate you on your publishing success!

Thanks for trusting us!

SECTION 1

Writing Children's Books

A Writer's Journey: Victoria Duerstock

Author of *Heart & Home* (Abingdon), *Heart & Home Christmas* (Abingdon), *Biblical Hospitality* (Skyhorse), and *Advent Devotions & Christmas Crafts for Families* (Skyhorse)

Tell us about the experience of getting your first Christian children's book published.

Because I have a current contract for an adult nonfiction book, I asked my editor if there would be any interest in a kid's version of my Heart & Home titles since I've had several readers share their desire for a title like that. My prior publishing house doesn't do kids titles, so I was free to ask the new house if they would. The answer was a hearty yes, but they wanted to get it contracted before the end of the year (less than two weeks away). It was a very quick process!

Chapter 1

Writing Christian Children's Books—It's a Calling
Michelle Medlock Adams

When I was in first grade, Mrs. True made an announcement that would forever change my life.

"We're having a poetry contest this week," she said, "so use today and tomorrow to come up with your best poem."

We had just studied the various types of poems, and I decided I really liked the ones that rhymed. In fact, I had checked out every book of rhyming poetry I could find from our school library, and I'd read them all—twice.

As my classmates wrote about their parents, grandparents, aunts and uncles, brothers and sisters, I carefully crafted the words to my poem: "I Love Penny."

Penny was my seven-year-old, pleasantly plump, wiener dog, and my best friend in the whole world.

My poem went a little something like this: "Penny is my very best friend. I'll love her to the very end. She's a very special wiener dog. I love her though she eats like a hog …"

OK, so I wasn't exactly a first-grade Dr. Seuss, but my poem was good enough to earn first prize. (I guess the other first-grade poets must've been really bad.) At any rate, I won a few sparkly pencils and the honor of going first in the lunch line that afternoon—and it was pizza day! Mrs. True also displayed my poem in the front of the room for all to see. I stared at my winning poem all afternoon. We'd moved on to another subject—history, I think—but I wasn't doing my assigned reading because I was too busy writing my follow-up poem, "The Big Yellow Sun," which went a little something like this: "The sun is so bright and full of power. If you leave your milk out, it'll turn it sour." (That's Newbery worthy right there, lol!)

That's the day I became a writer.

I wanted to write all the time, and so I did. I wrote during recess while other kids played tag and climbed on the monkey bars. I completely fell in love with words.

I wrote a play in fifth grade that we performed for all of the fifth-grade classes; I wrote short stories in junior high for a literary magazine, and I wrote many articles for my high school newspaper before majoring in journalism at Indiana University.

Though I began my career writing news stories for a daily paper, my career path took an unexpected turn when we moved to Texas so I could write features and personality profiles for an international ministry magazine. After a little while, the editor came to me and said, "You have kids, right?"

"Yes," I answered.

"Great, you can write some kids stories for our children's outreach."

I remember thinking, "Just because I have kids doesn't mean I know how to write for them."

But I was a journalist, so I began researching the world of writing for children, and once again, I fell in love. Head over heels. That was more than twenty years and one hundred books ago, and I've been lovesick ever since. Creating stories for children—stories that teach, entertain, encourage, and inspire—is my passion. It's a calling I don't take for granted, and neither should you.

No matter how you fell in love with writing for children, I'm just happy you did, and I'm happy you've picked up this book to learn from others on this same amazing journey. Let me encourage you to stay the course. Don't be discouraged by rejection letters. (I probably have enough to wallpaper my entire office!) Never think your work or your words are less important or less powerful simply because they are for children. Actually, they are more important and more powerful *because* they are for children.

You're a part of a very special club—a society of writers that woos children to fall in love with words and continue that love affair their whole lives through. You're the writer who transports children to far-off lands and make-believe worlds. You're the writer who causes children to dream a little bigger, laugh a little harder, feel a little deeper, and care a little more. You're a children's writer, crafting copy on the very hearts of your readers, so do it well and do it with passion.

This is your calling, and this is your time.

Chapter 2

What Makes a Great "High-Concept" Idea?
Cyle Young

High-concept ideas are all the rage these days, and as any author who has pitched to agents or editors can tell you, these industry experts often reject submissions and respond by saying the book isn't "high concept enough," or it's "*quiet.*" I'll be honest; it's hard always to know what the word *quiet* means in this scenario. But once you understand the principals behind high-concept ideas, you'll be able to limit those types of responses from industry professionals.

As a writer, you need to know how to write high-concept ideas and books to have the best chance of getting published and engaging readers. So, what do the words high-concept mean? High-concept books are books that catch your imagination. When you hear the premise behind a high-concept book, you're like, "Whoa!" There's this eureka moment that ignites a sense of wonder in your brain. When you come across a high-concept idea, you can't help but start thinking about the premise behind the idea. When you can't stop your mind from thinking about the idea—that's high concept. A great premise in a high-concept book will get the mind's attention long before a reader has ever even read the first word.

5 Qualities of High-Concept Ideas

1. A high-concept idea has a highly original concept or hook. When you write high-concept ideas, you want to build something that has a hook that gives someone that eureka moment. The lightbulb in their minds switches on, and you ignite a sense of wonder in their thoughts.

Some high-concept examples:

Orphan boy attends a school for wizards.
 —*Harry Potter* by J.K. Rowling
Underprivileged child wins a golden ticket to a whimsical candy factory.
 —*Charlie and the Chocolate Factory* by Roald Dahl
Samurai movie set in space.
 —*Star Wars* directed by George Lucas
A person's mind is the scene of the crime.
 —*Inception* directed by Christopher Nolan

These are just a few examples, but hopefully, you get the idea of original concept.

2. A high-concept idea asks a "what-if" question.
High-concept ideas question the norms of life and ask what would happen if the norms were twisted. Status quo is often shattered by the unique high-concept twist, but a high-concept idea needs also to be familiar enough that a

What Makes a Great "High-Concept" Idea?

reader has some sort of framework to engage with it.

Some high-concept examples:

What if there was an amusement park full of cloned dinosaurs, and they escaped?
—*Jurassic Park* by Michael Crichton
What if the Amish refugees had to launch into space to survive destruction, only to be confronted by vampires?
—*Amish Vampires in Space* by Kerry Nietz
What if the three little pigs were ninjas?
—*The Three Ninja Pigs* by Corey Rosen Schwartz
What if Peter Pan grew up and had a family?
—*Hook* directed by Steven Spielberg
What if you only had to work four hours each week and retire?
—*The 4-Hour Workweek* by Timothy Ferriss

You can see how these what-if scenarios twist the normal on its head. But you also can't help fantasizing about the interesting premises.

3. A high-concept idea has mass audience appeal.
High-concept ideas are too grandiose to be confined by genre or trope. They appeal to a wide readership in large genres, but even more preferably, their audience will span across multiple genres. The idea can't be too constrictive or weird that it won't resonate with a large audience.

Some high-concept examples:

A story about the survivors left behind after the rapture.
—*Left Behind* by Jerry Jenkins and Tim LaHaye
A love story between two teens dying of terminal cancer.
—*The Fault in Our Stars* by John Green

A comic book guide to surviving middle school
   —*Diary of a Wimpy Kid* by Jeff Kinney
Goldilocks visits the abode of three hungry dinosaurs.
   —*Goldilocks and the Three Dinosaurs* by Mo Willems

Publishers want books to fly off the shelves. They desire to sell hundreds of thousands of copies of high concept books, and they don't want them to sit on the shelf. The best way to sell a high number of copies is to publish a book that has appeal to the largest possible audience. Try to create a high-concept book that is also cross-genre.

4. A high-concept idea has a unique twist on the plot or premise.
Not every twist makes a book or idea high concept. Twists that only affect characters are not generally considered to be high concept; the twist needs to affect the plot or premise of the book.

Some high-concept examples:

Summer camp where the students are descendants of Greek gods.
   —*The Lightning Thief* by Rick Riordan
A Cinderella story set in modern LA.
   —*Pretty Woman* directed by Garry Marshall
Ferocious aliens invade the world, but they don't have eyes and track humans by echolocation.
   —*A Quiet Place* directed by John Krasinski
Teenagers fighting to death on television.
   —*The Hunger Games* by Suzanne Collins

When these twists come with high stakes, the high-concept idea can grab the reader's attention and keep them captivated on every page.

What Makes a Great "High-Concept" Idea?

5. A high-concept idea can be explained in one or two sentences.
You shouldn't need more than two sentences to explain a high-concept book. A high-concept book can be explained very easily because it should capture the reader immediately, even before they have opened up the book.

An unseen supernatural battle takes place in a small town.
   —*This Present Darkness* by Frank E. Peretti
Carrots conspire against a bunny that tries to eat them.
   — *Creepy Carrots* by Aaron Reynolds
Lord of the Rings meets the War of the Roses.
   — *A Game of Thrones* by George R. R. Martin
Elite teenage spy who falls in love with an ordinary boy.
   —*I'd Tell You I Love You, But Then I'd Have to Kill You* by Ally Carter

I don't generally recommend comparing your book to famous books unless it is a perfect comparison. It's hard to live up to the standard of famous works. George R. R. Martin did it successfully with his book series, but it isn't always an advisable strategy.

Ally Carter's book's title is high concept in and of itself. You can't help but wonder about the romance between the two characters. Whenever possible, strive to create compelling high-concept titles for your high-concept books.

High-concept ideas resonate with audiences from children's books, to nonfiction books, to fiction books. Start twisting the norm to create more amazing story and book ideas. Keep an idea journal and go out and observe life, nature, and people. You'll be amazed at how easily you will begin coming up with high-concept ideas once you start looking at life with a high-concept perspective.

Chapter 3

Writing Books That Make a Difference
Michelle Medlock Adams

I was in the window seat, thumbing through my recent issue of *Writer's Digest*, just waiting for the plane to take off when a mother and her young daughter sat down next to me.

"Don't worry, babe," the mom comforted. "You're going to be all right. We both will."

But the little girl didn't seem so sure. She fidgeted, hid her face in her stuffed unicorn, and eventually, her tears flowed.

She was afraid. Very afraid.

The mom in me wanted to help. I was so thankful I had listened to that still small Voice when I packed my briefcase that morning.

"Is this your first flight?" I asked the little girl.

Without looking at me, she nodded.

"It's a first flight for both of us," her mom quickly added. "And, we're both a little scared."

I locked eyes with the mama and asked, "I'm a children's author. Would it be OK if I shared a book with your daughter? I think it might be helpful."

"Of course," she answered.

I reached down and pulled out my book, *I Will Not Be Afraid* (Concordia Publishing House) and handed it to the little girl.

"I wrote this book for my little girls when they were afraid," I told her. "I want you to have it."

She looked up at me with her big brown teary eyes and gave me just a hint of a smile. She and her mama read every page and every accompanying Bible verse about fear, and by the time the plane took off, a calmness had blanketed our row.

That, my friends, is why we do what we do.

Our words, whether written in rhyme or narrative, hold great power. They can encourage, empower, educate, and comfort our readers. They can bring much-needed laughter, and they can provide a temporary escape into a world of story. As Christian writers for children, we can make a difference, and just knowing that fact makes all the difference. Knowing you're not just throwing together a manuscript for the sake of another sale, but rather you're crafting a story that might encourage a child who never receives any support at home, or that you're writing a book that could bring comfort to a scared little girl, that's what keeps us writing. That should be what drives us when we're putting in the hours—studying the craft, learning the market, revising and rewriting, praying over every word, and promoting—so our books can go every place they were intended to go and do the work they were destined to do.

Many publishers call these kinds of books "felt need" books, which basically means these children's books fill a void. They address a need, or they deal with a difficult situation in a very kid-friendly way. I love writing these kinds of books because it feels like ministry. You know why it feels that way? Because it is!

Some common felt-need topics include being afraid, being sad, feeling overwhelmed, feeling angry, and not feeling good enough. These types of needs can be narrowed down through story to address a very specific aspect of the felt need. For example, it's not just that the child is afraid. The child in your story might be afraid of the dark. That's a very common childhood fear. My daughter Abby was very afraid of the dark, which is why I wrote *Operation Moonbeam* (Little Lamb Books). Or it's not just that your main character feels sad, it's that she feels sad about her best friend moving away. Now, you've got the seeds of a story.

Felt-need books are also referred to as issue-oriented books. For example, there have been several books released in recent years about a grandparent's battle with dementia. It's very sad when Grandpa or Grandma no longer remember things. Helping a child understand the disease a little more and assuring the child that Grandpa's lack of memory certainly doesn't mean his love for the child is diminished, provides education and comfort to that reader. This can be handled through fiction or nonfiction, or you can combine the two by addressing the situation through story as well as providing nonfiction back matter about the disease and resources to learn more. (See Nancy I. Sanders' chapter on back matter.)

As I walked through Book Expo in New York City last year, I couldn't believe how many more companies had begun felt need/issue-oriented lines. Just as I walked into the main room at Book Expo, I saw a whole wall of board books that all began the same way, "When I feel ..." Do you know why these kinds of books are becoming more and more popular? I believe it's because they are becoming more and more needed. Kids today are facing adult situations, and as these little kids battle big problems, they often suffer anxiety, fear, anger, and hopelessness.

I'm not saying that as Christian children's writers we are expected to have all the answers, but I am saying this—we know the One who does! He can help us help them! And, it's our privilege to hold the little hands of our readers and walk them through these difficult seasons.

In order to do this with skill, however, we need to study others who have done it well. (See my chapter on Mentor Texts.) Here are just a couple of suggestions to get you started. Read *The Rough Patch* by Brian Lies to see a masterfully written children's book about dealing with grief. Read Crystal Bowman's book, *I Love You To the Stars— When Grandma Forgets, Love Remembers* that tackles the topic of dementia head-on. And, of course, you can check out *I Will Not Be Afraid* to see how I handled all of the most common childhood fears in one book.

Let me also challenge you to make a list of the things that most bothered you as a child or a teen. Was it anxiety over being bullied? Was it feeling embarrassed over not being good enough? Be specific when you make your list, attaching emotions to events or situations. Next, look at your list and ask, "Do children today face these same types of situations? Is there room on the shelf for another book addressing this topic or emotion? And, am I the one to write it?"

Once you've answered those questions, pray and ask God the best way to share your story, so the pain you experienced as a child (or the pain your own children have gone through) has purpose. Let it motivate you to write a life-changing book for children, or maybe just a comforting book for a little girl sitting next to you on your next flight. Be excited that God has chosen you for such a time as this ... your healing words are needed now more than ever.

So write.

> **Janet Surette**
>
> Janet Surette is an author and Bible teacher. She writes for women at janetsurette.com and is a contributing writer and speaker for The Gospel Coalition Canada in matters of Christian Living and Motherhood. She recently debuted in the Christian market with *Scarlett's Spectacles* by B&H Publishing.
>
> *What advice can you give to first-time authors?*
>
> BE PATIENT. The market moves very slowly. Send your best work and then fully engage your mind and effort in the regular things of life that God has entrusted to you. Otherwise, you'll drive yourself crazy and waste too much mental energy if you sit by the proverbial phone waiting for something to happen.
>
> *Do you have any nuggets of wisdom you can share about writing Christian children's books?*
>
> Don't be crippled by rejections. Not everyone sees the same thing when they look at a manuscript. It seemed that I couldn't win a conference contest to save my life and one lovely agent chose not to represent me because this agent didn't think my books would sell. Yet one of my contest-losing, un-sellable books was under contract about a

year later, with other manuscripts currently under consideration and a new contract pending. A rejection of a manuscript may not mean that your work is bad. It may simply mean that it's not what that agent or publisher was looking for at that particular season. Take any good advice given in those rejections, use it to strengthen your writing, and then carry on. The next person may see something very different in your writing and love it.

Are there any platform-building tips you can share to encourage other children's book authors?

Speaking is your book's best friend. If you have any inclination or giftedness to teach or speak in Christian circles, keep developing that ministry. Writing and speaking is a remarkably synergistic relationship: Speaking provides opportunities to sell books. Having a book published provides opportunities for more speaking engagements. That doesn't entirely make sense: Being a children's book author doesn't necessarily make you a better speaker, but people seem to perceive that it does. Being a Bible teacher to women doesn't necessarily mean that my children's book is good, but as I teach, I develop a rapport with my audience that always causes the book table to be notably busier after speaking than before. Attendees feel like they know me now, and they'll trust that my book is worthwhile if my teaching was biblical and beneficial.

Chapter 4

The Top Three Misconceptions for Writing in the Christian Children's Book Market
Michelle Medlock Adams

When speaking to writers at various SCBWI (Society of Children's Book Writers & Illustrators) events, I'm often asked the same questions regarding the Christian children's book market. It seems there are some common misconceptions about writing for children in the Christian market, so I thought we'd address those in this chapter.

Misconception #1: Children's stories in the Christian market should always teach a lesson.

Actually, children (as well as children's book editors) dislike preachy books. Good children's books, whether written for CRA (Christian Retail Association, the Christian market) or

ABA (American Booksellers Association, the non-Christian market), can teach a lesson as long as that message is woven throughout the text. You have to let the story drive the text, not the lesson. For example, Max Lucado's *You Are Special* picture book does a great job of communicating that important truth, but he does it through the story of Punchinello. In case you haven't read that story, Punchinello is a little wooden figure called a Wemmick. In the Wemmick world, Wemmicks spend their days giving stickers to good and not-so-good Wemmicks. If you're a good Wemmick, you get a gold star; if you're a not-so-good Wemmick, you receive a dot. When we encounter Punchinello, he is covered in dots and feeling really badly about it until he meets a Wemmick who has no stars or dots.

The no-dot/no-star Wemmick encourages Punchinello to visit Eli, the woodcarver, so he does. The Woodcarver explains to Punchinello that stars and dots only stick to you if you let them and that other people's opinions of him don't really matter because Eli—his maker—thinks Punchinello is very special. As Punchinello begins believing that he is special because of what Eli told him, a dot falls off of him.

So, without hitting the children over the head with an overt Bible lesson, this meaningful story of Punchinello and Eli beautifully conveys how special we are because God made us. The story has the message woven within its text—genius.

Misconception #2: The adult in the story should solve the problem.

Not true. Any adult in the story is simply a sidekick. The main character must be the child, and that child must solve the problem, whether we're talking about the CRA or ABA market.

The Top Three Misconceptions

When I judge writing contests or consult with new children's writers, this is probably the most common mistake I see.

Now, the main character can certainly take advice from an adult, but the child needs to do the problem solving. Why? Because through our books, we want to empower children, not tell them that adults must be present to solve their problems. We want to instill the message of "I can do all things through Christ who strengthens me"—in a sneaky, funny, kid-friendly way!

Misconception #3: One size fits all when it comes to Christian books.

Nope. Whether you're writing for the Christian market or the ABA market, every publisher has its own identity. In other words, just because your book is a good fit at one CRA publisher doesn't mean it will be a fit at all of them. I write for several different publishers in the Christian book world, but not every book I write is meant for all of those publishers.

For example, Concordia Publishing House (CPH) is a Lutheran publisher, and my editorial contact at CPH made it quite clear that Concordia didn't typically publish children's books featuring talking animals. With that knowledge, I knew that Concordia wouldn't be the future home for my talking animal series of Bible stories *(The Sparrow's Easter Song, Conversations On the Ark, Memories of the Manger,* and *Little Colt's Palm Sunday)* so I took those picture books to a different publisher and sold them. But I also knew that CPH did publish rhyming Bible stories as part of its ARCH Books, so I submitted "The Shepherds Shook in Their Shoes" for that line and got my foot in the door. After that, I went on to write four other ARCH books, a series of board books, and my award-winning picture book, *I Will Not Be Afraid.*

It's important that you don't just submit your work haphazardly; instead, spend time in your local library or at a Christian bookstore and investigate. Search for books like the manuscripts you've written and see what publishers put out those types of books. That's a good start to knowing where to submit your work. And, of course, a publisher's writer's guidelines will prove helpful, which can usually be found on that publisher's website. You'll also want to get copies of the most recent Writer's Market guides and attend any publishing panel offered at various writers conferences so that you'll be "in the know" concerning what each publisher is currently accepting and publishing.

Now that you know the truth, go forth and write great children's books!

An Editor's Journey

Peggy Schaefer
Associate Publisher
WorthyKids/Hachette Book Group

How many years have you worked in children's publishing, and how have you seen it change in recent years?

I worked with children's books on and off during the early part of my career, along with gift, travel, and inspirational adult. I've focused almost exclusively on children's books since 2007.

I think the landscape of the book market has changed tremendously in the last decade. We've lost physical retail space with major bookstore chains as well as smaller stores closing, and overall, much of the book business has moved online. Often, I'm asked how e-books have impacted my business. For the youngest age groups—board and picture books—I think the change has less to do with eBooks replacing print books and more to do with online shopping in general. As anyone who has ever searched for a book topic online and gotten twenty thousand-plus hits knows, it's a different experience to browse online than to walk through a store—and it requires a different business approach. There is also so much more competition for the reader's attention overall these days—even for children.

Are there key things you look for when you get a children's book proposal?

First and foremost, I look for something that moves me or excites me in some way—whether it touches my heart, introduces me to a new concept, or finds a new way of presenting an evergreen topic. And I also need to believe that our little readers will feel the same magic in the book. Of course, a well-written manuscript that shows an innate understanding of the reader is also of the utmost importance—things such as: Is the concept appropriate for the age group? Has the writer crafted a compelling story (no matter how simple)? Can children relate in some way to the characters? So that's what the editor/reader in me wants. From a business standpoint, I'm also looking for a well-prepared proposal that shows me the writer has done their homework and (1) knows that my publishing house is an appropriate match for the work, (2) is aware of what else is out in the market and can help me understand what sets this work apart from the rest, and (3) understands the importance and impact of self-marketing—whether through an author's social platforms or other relationships and marketing efforts.

What one piece of advice would you offer children's writers that would help them get published or find success with WorthyKids?

My mantra for would-be authors is *Shop! Read! Join!* While you may be able to write in a vacuum, you can't effectively market your work in a vacuum. You've got to spend time in bookstores or book departments and libraries to understand what is being published and who is publishing it. Use resources such as writer's guides, publisher websites, and industry newsletters to discover what individual publishers and editors are looking for. And join a writer's group to get critiques on your work and support along your journey.

Chapter 5

The Differences Between Age Groups
Cyle Young

What Are the Differences Between Age Categories?

The Children's/Juvenile Market goes from 0-18 years of age. Eighteen years is a massive age gap full of unique developmental milestones as children age. Publishers produce titles for each of these unique age groups specifically engineered to connect with the reader at his or her appropriate age level, concentration level, and comprehensive ability.

Be careful to adhere closely to these recommendations below. Publishers have standards for each of these categories, and you'll want to know exactly where your book fits in the juvenile market.

First Books

- Target Age Group is 0-2 years.
- Are often given before a baby is even born.
- Can be more complex because they are intended to be read by an adult to a child.
- Created so babies can hear and process words and concepts.

Board Books / Novelty Books

- Target Age Group is 0-3 years.
- Word Count is less than 100 words.
- Very thick pages made of cardboard so that children can play with them.
- Can be more complex because they are intended to be read by an adult to a child.
- Lots of images and simple words.
- Can include objects that stimulate a child's sense of touch or wonder.
- Read by a parent to a child with some interaction by the child.

Picture Books

- Target Age Group is 3-8 years.
- Word Count is up to 1,000 words, although 500 words is the current norm.
- Beautifully illustrated and generally 32 pages.
- Meant to be easy for a child to comprehend.
- Read between a parent and a child.
- Great illustration is a necessity.
- Can be rhythmic or prose.

Concept Books

- Target Age Group is 3-8 years.
- Word Count is up to 1,000 words.
- Teaches kids about the world surrounding them.
- Tackles sometimes difficult and challenging issues, ranging from learning to tie shoes to illness and death.
- Easy to understand and engaging for the child reader.

Early Readers

- Target Age Group is 5-8 years.
- Word Count is up to 3,000 words, but some publishers allow up to 5,000 words.
- Created for developing readers.
- Use simple words and easy to comprehend grammar.
- Often have only 4 to 6 words on each line of text to help with readability.
- Still includes illustrations along with the text.

Chapter Books

- Target Age Group is 7-10 years.
- Word Count is up to 10,000 words, but some publishers allow up to 12,000 words.
- Created for developing readers.
- Utilizes more complex words and grammar.
- Often have multiple chapters with longer paragraphs to ease children into reading.
- Typically sold in series.
- Illustrations are reduced to around one per chapter.

Middle Grade

- Target Age Group is 8-12 years.
- Word Count is between 15,000-50,000 words, although the category has been skewing longer recently. Fantasy books can be longer.
- Contains no profanity or graphic or persistent violence.
- Can be scary, but not horror.
- Romance is innocent and limited to crushes and first kisses.
- Main Characters are between the ages of 10 and 13 years old.
- Characters interact and react to their immediate world.
- Characters generally interact with family and friends.
- Books focus on real-life situations, typical of the target reader's everyday life, like forming friendships and dealing with bullies.

Young Adult Fiction

- Target Age Group is 13-18 years.
- Word Count is between 45,000-80,000 words. Fantasy books can be longer.
- Coarse language and violence are permissible.
- Romance is allowed and can be risqué in the general market.
- Main Characters are between the ages of 15 and 18 years old, but not generally in college.
- Characters grow up and move beyond just interactions with their family and friends.
- Characters self-reflect and analyze as they integrate into an unfamiliar world.

The Differences Between Age Groups

Board Books: Up to 100 words – Sweet spot: 50 words
Picture Books: 50 to 1,000 words – Sweet spot: 500 words
Early Readers: 1k–3k – Sweet spot: 1.2k
Chapter Books: 5k–12k – Sweet spot: 8k
Middle Grade: 15k–50k – Sweet Spot: 35k
Young Adult Fiction (YA): 50k–80k – Sweet Spot: 70k

Chapter 6

Writing and Publishing a Series
Ashley Jones

Since you're reading this book, you probably have several ideas floating around in your head. Some would make fun board books, while others would be great picture books. But sometimes an idea comes along that's too big for a single book. That's when you may want to consider writing a series.

Years ago, I came up with the idea of a picture-book series in which farm animals asked faith-based questions and discovered biblical answers. I started writing and, after a while, I had covered six topics: God, prayer, love, forgiveness, church, and heaven. I dubbed the series Big Answers, and my agent and I went shopping for a publisher. Thankfully, Little Lamb Books believed in the project and contracted for all six books! The first book, *Who Is God?* will debut in 2021. I was so excited when a traditional publisher picked up the series and we started editing the first two books. Unfortunately, COVID-19 hit, the publisher had to reevaluate their lineup, and my series was canceled. Now my agent is shopping the series once again.

As a new writer, I'm learning the ins and outs of publishing children's books; it's literally on-the-job training! This setback has certainly been disheartening, but I did learn a lot during the editing process. Now I can appreciate the difference between publishing a stand-alone children's book and a series. Before you tackle a series, here are some aspects you should consider.

Theme or Topic
Books in a series must be linked together by theme or topic.

If the books are simple, a general topic can be used to pull them together. My son has a touch-and-feel board-book series in which each book features a different group of animals, from baby animals to zoo animals. The overall topic is simply animals.

In a story-driven picture-book series, an overarching theme can be used to pull the books together. In Big Answers, the characters on the farm discover biblical answers to questions of faith. Each book has its own topic and theme (e.g., God listens to our prayers, God forgives us), but the theme that connects them all is that God loves us and wants to be with us.

To determine your theme, ask yourself, "What is the one thing I want kids to learn from this series?"

Story and Style
The storyline and the style of the books should be consistent throughout the series.

In my book *Who Is God?* Fritzy the squirrel is adopted by the farmer's dogs. In the next book, *What Is Love?* Fritzy participates in a game the other animals are playing. The publisher and I discussed releasing *What Is Love?* first, but that would have required a rewrite of the story to avoid a logic conflict: having Fritzy on the farm before she was found and adopted. We decided to stick with the original order.

Besides being logical, the story should also feel cohesive, and that's where style comes into play. Illustrations are very important in any children's book, but in a series, you also need continuity. Ideally, you'll have the same illustrator for the whole series, but that's not always the case. Regardless, you'll want to make sure your characters—how they act and what they do—are consistent throughout the series. For example, in *Who Is God?* I described Muffin the cat as "snaggle-toothed" and wrote how she "slinked away" at the end of a scene. The editor asked if we should soften the language, and I explained that Muffin is the instigator on the farm and that her bad behavior is key to the plot of a later book. We decided to keep the original language, and a note was made for the illustrator.

The style of the manuscript is also important. If the first book is written completely in rhyme, then the remaining books should rhyme in the same way. Other elements, such as the presence and amount of dialogue and rhythm should be used consistently throughout the series.

Once you've written your series, read through it from beginning to end in one sitting, identifying anything that is illogical or feels out of place—because parents and kids will definitely pick up on it too. Make sure each book stands alone and that it contributes to the series as a whole.

Publishing

It's harder to publish a series than a stand-alone book.

I'm very fortunate that a traditional publisher believed in the vision of Big Answers and contracted for the whole series.

It's more common these days for publishers to contract only one book with the option to buy the rest of the series. If the book underperforms, though, the publisher may reject the remaining books. Depending on the terms of your contract, that could mean the death of your series.

I was so excited when my first publisher contracted for the whole Big Answers series! However, when they took a financial hit due to COVID-19, it was my series that got canceled. This can be very frustrating, but it's important to remember that publishers make a large investment in each book they publish. And when it comes to a series, they're also investing in you, the author. While the publisher may hope and believe the series will do well and that you'll promote it as best you can, they may not be ready to risk their financial outlook on it. This is why it's far more common for publishers to contract only one book with the option to buy the rest of the series if the first book performs well.

Before you sign a publishing contract—whether it's for a series or a standalone book—have your agent or attorney review the terms with you.

Marketing
A series creates marketing leverage.

Both kids and adults love series, and that's great news! If you can impress your readers with your first book, they'll be more likely to buy the second book, the third book, and so on. This is especially true if you have vivid characters or a continuing storyline because children naturally want to know what happens next.

As soon as your first book releases, create marketing leverage using your email newsletter. Encourage readers to sign up by providing free lead magnets (like teaching tools). Then email your followers whenever you have an upcoming release—they'll be glad you did!

My favorite children's books feature animals, so I envisioned the "kids" in my books as young animals on a farm. Later on, I learned that many Christian publishers refuse stories in which animals speak or pray. While they may allow animals in the illustrations, they won't accept any text that says something like, "Betty the cow said …" I tried, but I couldn't think of a way to rewrite my series using human kids. Fortunately, I found a publisher who didn't mind using animals in the story—they even preferred it! And I trust I'll find another publishing house that feels the same way. So my rule is, if you can steer away from animals talking, then great, but if you can't, then pray about it and wait. Still, if you can avoid having animals talking in your story, it will open up your publishing opportunities.

Chapter 7

Storytelling for Children
Steven James

Telling a great story is more than simply relating what happens or explaining things that occur in order. The story's first event isn't just the one that comes first chronologically, but the one that *originates* all that follows. The final event isn't just the last one, but the *culminating* event of the story.

Think of a story as a transformation unveiled—either the transformation of a character, his situation, or a relationship he has.

Stories revolve around characters who are pursuing something that matters to them, so when you're diving into your story, rather than ask, "What should happen next?" ask, "What does this character want right now?"

Often, a story will show the normal life of the character before including a crisis or calling event that disrupts her life and initiates the story's central struggle.

Then the tension or complications escalate as the character tries to accomplish, avoid, or obtain something. Finally, after working through setbacks that move the story forward, the character will typically find new insights or a new situation that results from facing the struggle, making a meaningful choice, and accomplishing what he set out to do.

A good example of how this works can be found in the well-known story of "Samuel's Calling" in 1 Samuel 3. The chapter begins by showing normal life for Samuel and for God's people: "In those days the word of the Lord was rare; there were not many visions … Now Samuel did not yet know the Lord: The word of the Lord had not yet been revealed to him," (vv. 1, 7 NIV).

So, the word of the Lord and visions from him were rare, Israel didn't have a prophet to tell them God's word, and Samuel didn't yet know the Lord.

Then comes the story's disruption when something extraordinary happens on an ordinary night: The Lord speaks to Samuel, giving him a message that he's supposed to take to Eli.

But there's a complication, a struggle inside of Samuel, and in the morning, he resists at first by going back to work doing his normal duties rather than accomplishing the mission God had called him to do: "Samuel lay down until morning and then opened the doors of the house of the Lord. He was afraid to tell Eli the vision" (v. 15).

Samuel was afraid of doing God's will because he thought something bad might happen if he did. It's a common struggle that all of us can identify with!

However, in the end, when Eli confronts him, Samuel makes a choice that leads to a change. He delivers the message God had commissioned him to share, and both the condition of the Israelites and his own relationship with the Lord were changed: "The Lord was with Samuel as he grew up, and he let none of Samuel's words fall to the ground. And all Israel from Dan to Beersheba recognized that Samuel was attested as a prophet of the Lord. The Lord continued to appear at Shiloh, and there he revealed himself to Samuel through his word" (vv. 19-21).

At the end of the story, the problems that introduced the chapter are resolved: (1) God has a new spokesperson; (2) Samuel now knows the Lord; (3) God's word has been revealed to him, and as a result, (4) Samuel is faithful in sharing God's word with the people.

See the transformations and how the end of the story reveals them?

Remember, in a story, readers will identify with the character who has the struggle, not the one with all the answers. (Check it out by reading Jesus's parables. It's true in every one of them!) So, in this story, children will naturally identify with Samuel rather than Eli.

By the way, a common weakness of "Christian" stories for children has the main character (usually a child about the age of the story's readers) go to a kind and wise adult who gives her advice or answers that will solve all her problems if only she'll just put them into practice. At first, she resists, and things get worse. Then, at the climax, she does, and everything is solved.

Don't fall into this trap. Let the discovery come from within the character and not from someone else showing up to solve the problem (through what they say or do) on her behalf.

Children love surprises, funny situations, action, interesting characters who do intriguing things, and adventures that they can take in their imaginations. So, as you begin your story, think through who your main character is, what she wants, and what's getting in the way of her obtaining it.

Try to include struggles your readers will be able to identify with. For instance, feeling lonely or left out, being scared, hoping to find a new friend at school, wondering if you'll ever get along with your siblings, being tempted to lie or get away with something that you know you shouldn't do, being selfish, or not wanting to share.

So, as you explore your story idea, ask yourself these ten key questions:

1. What is normal life like for this character at the beginning of the story?
2. What happens to disrupt that? How does she respond?
3. What does she want, and how does she try to get life back to normal?
4. What complications or struggles make things worse?
5. How is she forced to make a difficult decision at the climax that determines the end of the story?
6. Will children identify with the main character's struggle?
7. How is the main character (or her situation) different at the end of the story?
8. Have I avoided having an authority figure or answer-giver solve the main character's struggle for her?
9. What truths will children take away from this story?
10. Does the story honor God by celebrating what He celebrates?

Chapter 8

Know Your Audience
Rachel Pellegrino

Audience. Those readers that enjoy picking up our books and reading each word, each page, each title. We all want as many readers as possible in our audience. But do you really know your audience? Do you know who will be reading your book? Who is spending their dollars to buy your book? It's easy to get excited about writing your manuscript, but in order for you to have true success, you must know your audience inside and out.

As a writer for the Christian juvenile market, whether fiction or non-fiction, your audience is actually more layered than the children in a half-moon circle at your feet during a reading. It's necessary that you not only identify your audience, but that you also understand what's important to them, what their world revolves around, and what appeals to them, so you can adapt your tone, vocabulary, theme, and content to their interests. Knowing your audience, whether you write an elementary picture book or a young adult novel, will help you effectively communicate with them and build a dedicated audience for the future.

Let's talk specifically about our audience within two categories: Readers and Buyers.

The first question you need to be able to answer is **Who Will Be Reading Your Book?** Your readers are made up of a variety of ages, locations, preferences, and backgrounds. Are they kindergarteners learning their letters and how to write words? Are they fourth-grade students who are starting to question their parents and looking to fit in among their classmates? Are they attending a public middle school and being impacted by their peers and searching for validation each day? Are they high school homeschool students driving themselves, getting their first job, and preparing to graduate?

For each story, character, or theme that you focus on, remembering who your readers are, what relates to them, and what grabs their attention will bring you closer to writing a strong manuscript.

The second question is **Who Is Buying Your Book?** Your audience is never made up *only* of readers. Along with those who read the story are those who are going to spend the money to purchase your book, and as a writer, you must always consider WHO they are. For instance, are they any of the following:

- Family - Parents, Grandparents, Siblings, Aunts, Uncles, etc.
- Educators - Teachers, Principals, Librarians, Homeschool Co-ops, etc.
- Vendors - Bookstores, Gift Shops, Coffee Houses, Theaters, Restaurants, etc.
- Churches – Pastors, Youth Pastors, Children's Ministry Leaders, etc.

> Influencers – Mommy Bloggers, Magazine Listers, Contest Judges, etc.

Notice that within each category, there are more layers, and within each of these layers, each one of these audiences is going to pick up your book, read your words, view the illustrations, and assess whether or not it's a good buy for their children, their customers, their congregation, or their clients.

Trying to determine which of these audiences is most important to you can be daunting, but it doesn't have to be. They are all important but in different ways. Instead of letting your fear of getting the audience wrong dominate your thoughts, there are three ways you can really know each of your audiences and write a book that is perfect for all of them.

Research

Before you write a manuscript that will land an agent or publishing house and find its way to bookstore shelves, you need to do your research.

If you have friends with kids in the age group you want to write in, spend time with them.

Chat about what they and their kids are interested in. Visit with teachers and find out what stories are a part of their curriculum. Volunteer at your local library and chat with the librarian about titles they can't keep on their shelves. Offer to spend a Sunday morning once a month in your children's ministry and find out what topics, trends, and themes they are focusing on for their lessons. Sit in a local bookstore and look at how they shelve the books for your genre and where customers gravitate to during their visit. All of these moments combine to allow you to really see the mindset of the readers and the buyers.

Read

There is popular advice shared often at conferences: *Read What You Want to Write*. I don't know who originated the saying, but they were wise beyond their years.

Go now to your local library and gather up a bundle of books in the age group that you want to write. What's on the shelves? What point of view is used most often? What's the book's word count? What themes are trending? What social issues are prominently displayed? What character traits are found most often? What holidays are more readily available than others?

When you're done with that stack, go back and do it again. Really spend time learning what makes up a good picture book or middle grade or young adult novel ... and what doesn't.

If you aren't sure where to begin looking, libraries usually have a reading list from local school districts that use a mix of classics and newer titles. You can also check out the latest award winners, including Caldecott and Newbery winners. Or, you could visit the Association for Library Service to Children's website and view a variety of reading lists they have compiled.

Reading within the genre and age group you want to write in allows you to experience what your audience is experiencing already, see who your competition is, and see where you can fit best. It also allows you to get a sense of the vocabulary used, the general word counts per genre, and the trends in literature.

Connect

Once you've researched your audiences and read the books already published in your genre, you, dear writer, must *connect* to your audience and what they need, believe, feel, and expect. Connecting with your audience requires that the reader find something in your story to zero in on and feel they can relate to. Maybe it's a family dynamic or a physical trait in one of your primary or secondary characters. Possibly it's a hobby or a sport the main character is involved in throughout the story. Maybe it's an interest in trains, dragons, or the color pink.

Whatever it is, make sure that there is something specific that the reader can connect with and leave them talking about it with others.

And, take what you've learned and connect with your buyer. For instance, can you answer these questions:

- Will it enhance a homeschool parent's curriculum?
- Will it be a visual aid for a youth pastor?
- Will it be a birthday gift from a grandparent to a child?
- Will it tie into a holiday event for a bookseller?
- Will it sit on an art gallery shelf?

If so, you're connecting to your buying audience and how they sell and market your story, which means you've met the needs of those who will give it the best chance at discovery.

Your Christian children's or YA book is going to attract a certain audience based on its content, cover, price point, title, theme, and more details that you don't necessarily have total control over during the publishing process. However, the one thing you have absolute control over is who you write for, and if you **know your audience**, you can help your story, and you be successful *and* profitable.

Chapter 9

Injecting a Dose of Humor into Your Children's Book
Doug Peterson

Humor is hard work.

I have written both serious and humorous fiction and nonfiction for preschool through adult readers in all types of genres and mediums, from books and plays to magazine articles and comic books. But out of all of this work, humor is the hardest.

As the writer G. K. Chesterton once said, it's much easier to take oneself seriously than to be lighthearted. "For solemnity flows out of men naturally," he wrote. "But laughter is a leap. It is easy to be heavy: hard to be light. Satan fell by the force of gravity."

I used to write zany picture books for VeggieTales, the animated vegetables who sing silly songs, dodge slushies being hurled at them from the walls of Jericho, and wonder where oh where is their hairbrush. So, if you're looking to inject humor into your children's writing, let me go through my process when working on a VeggieTales story. Hopefully, you might be able to glean some ideas from this process and adapt them to whatever kind of children's book you might be writing.

When working on a VeggieTales story, I always began by getting myself in a silly frame of mind. As anyone familiar with the VeggieTales series knows, silliness reigns supreme, with "Silly Songs With Larry" being its most popular feature. So my first recommendation to anyone who wants to lighten up their children's book is …

Do Some Silly Mental Warm-ups. Before you run a marathon, you train. And before you write a humorous children's book, you fill your head with goofiness. The way I did that was to sit down and watch a couple of VeggieTales videos. This got my silly juices flowing.

So figure out what gets you laughing and do that before you begin. For example, try picking out your favorite zany children's book, whether it might be *Cloudy With a Chance of Meatballs*, *Green Eggs and Ham*, or any one of the multitude of funny books out there.

Once I was feeling lighthearted, then it was on to brainstorming ideas. In the case of VeggieTales, my next step was …

Create the Nugget of Truth. When writing for VeggieTales, we were encouraged to begin with a "nugget of truth"—a one-sentence description of the story's theme. This sentence should be so simple that a preschooler can understand it.

For the very first VeggieTales video of all time—*Where's God When I'm S-Scared?*—the nugget was very simple: "God is bigger than the boogy man." Anyone can understand that idea. I co-wrote the story for one VeggieTales video,

Larry-Boy and the Rumor Weed, and its nugget of truth was: "God wants us to spread nice words." The nugget doesn't need to be clever—just clear and concise.

Once I had that nugget of truth in place, it was time to …

Discover the Big Idea. There's a reason the company that produced VeggieTales was called Big Idea. When it comes to any kind of writing, the Big Idea is the key. Therefore, brainstorming ideas was roughly 80 percent of my work on a VeggieTales book.

Humor comes in many different forms, so tailor your brainstorming process to your particular project. In the case of VeggieTales, many of the stories are spoofs, so that's where my mind went. For example, Larry-Boy is a spoof on Batman, as this silly superhero battles villains who personify various sins. In the first Larry-Boy video, the caped cucumber battles the giant Fib, who represents lying.

When I brainstormed ideas for the second Larry-Boy video, I tried to figure out what kind of villain might personify gossip. Gossip is something that spreads, so I tried to think of things that spread. Fire spreads, but that's too violent. Peanut butter spreads, but it's too sticky.

Then it came to me—weeds spread—and so that became my Big Idea. Larry-Boy would battle a villain who begins as a single, small, innocent weed. Similarly, gossip begins with one small, nasty rumor, but then it spreads and grows—like weeds. So Larry-Boy would battle the ominous Rumor Weed.

Many of the books that I wrote for VeggieTales were also spoofs, such as my personal favorite, the Mess Detectives series. In these books, Bob the Tomato and Larry the Cucumber play *Dragnet*-style detectives, investigating messes that kids get themselves into.

Which leads me to another step in the process …

Give Parents Something to Laugh About. One of the secrets of VeggieTales' success, or Pixar's for that matter, is that the stories work on different levels for people of different ages. The stories can be grasped by the very youngest, but there are also sly references that only adults can pick up.

In my Mess Detective books, Bob and Larry are detectives modeled after the old *Dragnet* TV series. The series is so old that many parents today probably aren't aware of it, although grandparents may recall it. But that's OK. You don't have to understand the *Dragnet* references to enjoy a Mess Detectives story.

For instance, in *Dragnet*, Sergeant Joe Friday always said, very seriously, "I carry a badge." In the Mess Detectives, Larry the Cucumber says, equally seriously, "Bob carries a badge. I carry a badger. Don't ask why."

Readers don't have to know this *Dragnet* reference. The fact that Larry carries a stuffed badger everywhere he goes, instead of a police badge, is just the kind of silly thing he would do—and that's all the readers really need to know. If a parent or grandparent catches the *Dragnet* reference, all the better.

Speaking of spoofs, another tactic that I used in crafting silly stories was to …

Mix and Match Worlds. By this, I mean, I would mix bits and pieces of the contemporary world with the historical. VeggieTales stories are set in many different historical periods—biblical settings, the Old West, knights, pirates, Vikings, etc. But in each of these settings, contemporary references abound.

For instance, some VeggieTales stories take place in the Old West, but Veggie cowboys hurl dodge balls at each other, rather than draw guns on each other. Real guns have no place in VeggieTales stories, so they are replaced with something kids can relate to—dodge balls. This is only fitting because one of the most famous of Wild West locations was Dodge City. Hence, Dodge Ball City.

In *King George and the Ducky*, VeggieTales even managed to tackle the tricky story of David and Bathsheba by mixing and matching. In the Bible story, King David desired Bathsheba, so he found a way to steal her from her husband. In *King George and the Ducky*, King George is greedy for rubber duckies, so he steals a rubber ducky from the brave soldier, Thomas.

Mixing and matching dodge balls with cowboys, or rubber duckies in Bible stories works for VeggieTales. You have to decide whether it fits your style of book.

At last, when all of the brainstorming is done, then comes the final step …

Sit Down and Write! Writer's block is no laughing matter, but if you do your job in the brainstorming stage, wrestling those words onto the page will be much less painful. When you do your prep work properly, the humor will seem to leap from the page as if gravity can't hold it down.

> "It takes a heap of sense to write good nonsense."
>
> Mark Twain

Melody Delgado

Do you have any nuggets of wisdom you can share about writing Christian children's books?

While we are striving to impart wisdom, and that's important, books for children also need to be entertaining. Making children laugh is always a good goal, but writing an engaging story is crucial.

What has been your greatest joy in your publishing journey?

Holding a copy of my book in my hands.

What has been your greatest struggle in your publishing journey?

Getting copies into libraries. Librarians sometimes have limited ways to purchase books.

Chapter 10

Breathe New Life into an Old Concept
Michelle Medlock Adams

One of the biggest challenges of writing for children is figuring out how to put a new twist on an old storyline. Once you accomplish that as a writer, it's a true thing of beauty and brilliance. That's what Adam Rex did with his book, *School's First Day of School* (Roaring Brook Press). In this charming story, Rex breathes new life into a tired topic by shifting the perspective from the child's point of view to the school building's POV. Children get to experience all of the same emotions they might be feeling as a new school year approaches—excitement, fear, anticipation, embarrassment, dread, and more—but through the eyes of the school building.

Boom.

Just like that, we have a fresh perspective on the old concept. Literally, hundreds of books have been written on that topic. In fact, I wrote one called, *My First Day of School* (WorthyKids) in 2017, and though I like how it turned out, it's certainly not as clever or compelling as *School's First Day of School*.

That's a perfect example of thinking outside the box for that different twist. *Publisher's Weekly* thought so, too, stating the following in its review: "Every so often, a book comes along with a premise so perfect, it's hard to believe it hasn't been done before; this is one of those books."

Let me give you another example of how a gifted author friend of mine took what could have been a straightforward, boring biography about two well-known historical figures but instead crafted copy that's touching hearts around the world. It's a book called *Martin & Anne* by my friend Nancy Churnin. In *Martin & Anne* (Creston Books), readers are taken on a journey that explores the lives of Martin Luther King, Jr. and Anne Frank—two history makers born the same year on different continents. Churnin details how both faced discrimination from the time they were very young. Martin Luther King, Jr. faced "Whites only" signs while Anne Frank grew up facing "No Jews allowed" policies. They were kindred spirits who suffered untimely deaths yet impacted the world during their time on this earth.

Do you see what Churnin did so brilliantly here? Can you identify the twist? Instead of writing the typical biography, she created a type of comparison/contrast book, paralleling the lives of these two extraordinary people—Martin & Anne. She didn't write a chronological retelling of Martin Luther King, Jr.'s life, nor did she write just another ordinary biography about Anne Frank. She found a new way to share important details about these two historical figures' lives. This book is more than clever; it's inspired.

Bible Story Retellings

When I decided early in my career that I wanted to write a series of Bible stories for children, I knew I wanted to retell those stories in a new, engaging way. I wanted to "Go tell it on the Mountain" but I wanted to tell it in a way the children on "that mountain" might never have heard before. I wanted children to *want* to know more about the Bible. I wanted to make it so fun that they'd reach for my books just as often as they reached for Dr. Seuss's books. After all, no disrespect to Dr. Seuss (love him!), but knowing the story of Easter is way more important than knowing about the Whos living in Whoville. So, I set out to make the retelling of some of the most beloved Bible stories freshly come to life. I knew that children loved animals because I'd been volunteering in the library at my daughters' elementary school for quite some time, and all of the animal books—fiction and nonfiction—were constantly in demand. That was my "aha moment."

What if I tell these Bible stories from an animal's perspective, an animal that might've been present during these events?

So, that's what I did when I wrote *Conversations On the Ark, Memories of the Manger, Little Colt's Palm Sunday*, and *The Sparrow's Easter Song* (Ideals Children's Books). In *Conversations on the Ark*, all of the animals are discussing why they are on this big boat … and what is rain? And, is this Noah guy a loon? The dialogue between the animals makes for some funny moments, yet the facts of the story are intact. It's just a different way of telling the story of Noah's Ark.

In *Memories of the Manger* an old dove who was present the night Jesus was born shares with all the baby animals about the events that took place right there in that very stable. In *Little Colt's Palm Sunday* we hear from the colt who ends up carrying Jesus on his back—a pretty big mission for such a little, inexperienced colt. He'd never been ridden before that big day! I include all of the facts of the Palm Sunday Bible story, but also, I weave in the thread that God can use you for big things, even though you're little. And, in *The Sparrow's Easter Song* a sparrow who witnesses the death and resurrection of Jesus tells all of her animal friends about the miracle that's occurred, which brings hope to the land and a new song to the sparrow's heart. (Ironically, *The Sparrow's Easter Song* came out at the same time the movie, *The Passion of the Christ*, debuted. And, if you remember, that movie—because of its graphic nature—was not recommended for children. So I was able to offer my book as an alternative way of sharing such an important story in a less gory, less scary way.)

So, how can you put a new twist on a tired tale?

- Force yourself to think outside the box by asking lots of "I wonder" questions. (I wonder if that little colt was scared to carry the Son of God on his back?)
- Never accept your first thoughts about how to tell the story.
- Explore several options, sharing the story from various points of view, and see which version is stronger.
- Write your story in both rhyme and narrative and see which is better.
- Don't settle for a story that's good enough. Aspire to create a brilliant story.
- Look for the little-known details about common stories and see if you can build on those facts to create a unique book that will wow the editors of *Publisher's Weekly*, and more importantly, inspire a new generation of readers.

Chapter 11

Writing Strong Characters
Nancy I. Sanders

Need help developing strong characters? The kind young readers can relate to, root for, and remember long after reading your book? Start incorporating play sessions into your normal writing routine where you explore your characters' world. Your characters will never be the same!

Children like to play. Play is essential to learn the skills needed to mature into adulthood. As children's writers, it's important to incorporate times of play into our writer's day. This directed play will help us develop skills needed to achieve success in today's publishing world.

Here are several "games" to play, and writing exercises to do, to help you develop a strong cast of characters for today's current Christian market.

Stereotype Mix and Match

As you're developing your cast of characters, make a list of stereotypical biblical characters such as Apostle Paul the zealot, King David the man after God's own heart, and Jacob the deceiver. Then choose three of these stereotypes to combine into a brand-new character. For example, you could have a teen who is a staunch and outspoken atheist but experiences an eventful conversion (like the Apostle Paul), becomes a Christian musician with a heart after God (like King David), yet has to deal with his tendency to lie and cheat (like Jacob). Mixing and matching stereotypes such as these can give you a very strong character with a fresh and unique twist.

Animal Traits

Make a list of animals and their stereotypical traits. Such as a beautiful Irish setter who always wins blue ribbons at dog shows, a giraffe who is taller than all the other animals, and a lion who is king of the jungle. Or a strong but not-too-bright bulldog, a pampered Persian cat, and a parrot who repeats everything she hears. Then assign a specific animal and its traits to each character in your story. For example, your main character could be like an Irish setter. Beautiful. Talented. A "purebred" with a history of famous ancestors. Successful at everything she does. But like all purebreds, she struggles with an inherited weakness. A secondary character could be like a parrot. Smart. Loud. A gossip. Always sitting on a perch nearby, commenting about what's going on around her, but never actually getting involved in the action.

Spiritual Gift Bag

Make a list of spiritual gifts using 1 Corinthians 12:4-11, Romans 12:4-8, and Ephesians 4:11-13 as a guide. Assign each of your characters at least one strong spiritual gift and give some of your characters a second or third spiritual gift as well. Even villains in your story can be assigned a spiritual gift that they misuse. Play around with the results by writing a few scenes and seeing how your characters act and speak based on their own personal bag of spiritual gifts.

Personification

Playing this "game" helps each of your characters develop a strong voice and unique personality. In the next scene you plan to write in your manuscript, replace each character with a stereotypical forest animal such as a rabbit, a fox, an owl, and a wolf. Write the first draft of that scene with these animals. How will each one handle the conflict? What unique voice will each one speak with?

The rabbit will be shy and quickly run off when trouble brews. The fox will be sneaky, perhaps lying about his involvement. The owl will give wise advice and figure out how to best handle the plot conflict. The wolf will be mean … and loud … and threaten to call in the rest of his gang to help bully his way around if things aren't going his way.

After you write that draft, step back a moment, and evaluate your creative process. Was it easy for each character to act and speak in a distinctive and strong way?

Yes! Of course.

Why?

Because you automatically knew a lot about them.

This is the same depth we need to know our characters we're writing about, whether it's for picture books or young adult novels, fiction or nonfiction. If we know our characters like we know a cast of simple woodland creatures, we'll know how they'll handle conflict (or not) and act or react in a scene. We'll know their unique voice and the things they'll say, so when we're writing each of their dialogues, it will come through as authentic.

As children's writers, there are various strategies we can use to know our characters better. We can "interview" them to discover their likes and dislikes, their strengths and weaknesses, their habits and personal quirks. We can give each of our characters a backstory, putting together an entire memory book for them much as a parent does for her child. Through the process, we will learn more about their parents, their close family members such as brothers and sisters, their childhood experiences, and the places they live in, such as their home, neighborhood, school, and church they attend.

We can make simple sketches of their bedroom, clubhouse, or favorite place to spend their time. What color and theme will they decorate it (or not!)? What books will they have, if any? Will there be one or two favorite toys they kept from their younger years? Get out your crayons and markers, or art supplies your target audience would be using, and illustrate your character's world. Nothing fancy. Just have fun!

Even though much of their backstory or setting details will never make it into the actual text of the manuscript you're writing, you'll have added depth to your character that wasn't there before. This helps your character feel like a real person kids will really want to know (and read more about!).

This week and in the weeks ahead, as you're planning your writing routine, schedule in play dates with your characters. Take time to know your characters better. The results will help bring them to life and create strong, memorable characters kids love.

Chapter 12

Writing Back Matter That Matters
Nancy I. Sanders

Pick up a nonfiction book for kids and flip to the back. Chances are you'll find a glossary, timeline, or map. Sometimes you'll see a puzzle, craft, or devotion. In publishing jargon, this extra material found after the main body of the book is called "back matter." Back matter can add depth and interest to your nonfiction manuscript.

Including back matter in your nonfiction proposal can help catch an editor's eye and land a contract. It's easy to add to the end of your manuscript. Just give each section an appropriate heading and type it to follow after the main body of your manuscript. An extra perk about back matter is that you are not limited by word count. Sometimes back matter is longer than the picture book's main text! When submitting my manuscript, I often include two word counts: the main text and the back matter.

When you're preparing to write the back matter, include a research and brainstorming session for ideas on which kind of back matter to include. On any given manuscript, at this stage of writing, I'll get several tote bags and visit my local library. I walk up and down the children's nonfiction aisle and collect a variety of children's nonfiction books in my tote bags. At home, I lay them all out on a large table and divide them up according to the type of back matter they include. Then I read through the back matter in the various books and choose my favorite examples to use in my own particular project. Here are some of my favorites:

Author's Note

This is the place you get to tell the whole story behind the story. In today's picture book market that often limits text to fewer than 1,000 words (and often as low as 500 words), as an author, you're under tight restrictions to tell a short concise story, often focusing on one significant event. In the Author's Note, however, you can use as many words as you need to explain your topic's complete story. I've even seen Author's Notes that cover two or three pages full of tiny text!

Timeline

When creating a timeline, try to include each entry of the same level of importance. If you're writing a biography, a birth to death timeline might be best, including eight to ten significant events. If writing about an important historic event, start and end the timeline with a key event related to your topic.

Glossary

A glossary is a dictionary of keywords found in your manuscript. Ten to twenty keywords are usually sufficient. Most publishers prefer highlighting the first time each entry appears in your manuscript's text. I keep a children's school dictionary for reference while I'm writing the definitions. When writing a beginning reader or book that elementary children will be reading by themselves, I use the *Children's Writer's Word Book* by Alijandra Mogilner to choose grade-appropriate words.

Bibliography

I often include a "Selected Bibliography" with a dozen or so of the key research books I used. Many publishers use the *Chicago Manual of Style* as the format for a bibliography. If in doubt, check other books by the publisher you're targeting and format your bibliography accordingly.

Endnotes, Footnotes, or Source Notes

Sometimes a Christian publisher wants to produce nonfiction books that meet educational standards. One of these standards is to include quotes in the main text with an endnote, footnote, or source note identifying the book and page number where that quote was found. A perk of writing to support educational standards such as the Common Core is that it can open doors for Christian books to be added to classroom or public school libraries or to be used by students as research material for writing reports.

Biographies of Bible Heroes

If you're writing a nonfiction book that includes a lot of people from the Bible, it can be helpful to include a biography section in the back matter with short biographies of key names. Bible dictionaries are helpful for reference when writing a biography such as this in your back matter. Plus, it gives a handy guide for young readers to refer to as they're reading through the book.

Activities or Puzzles

Nonfiction is a great genre for adding activities or puzzles in the back matter. Science experiments, historic recipes, crossword puzzles, or word search puzzles are just a few of the ideas you can use. Look in the back of current published books for even more activities you can include in today's digital age, especially as kids get more device-savvy at even younger ages.

Resources for Young Readers

Kid-friendly websites to explore, children's books for further reading, and places kids can visit are key ingredients for this section of your back matter. If you plan to create a website for your published book, I always recommend listing your book's website in the published book as a place to go to find kid-friendly websites. By putting these URLs on your own website instead of in the published book, you avoid the problem of having links stop working or sites changing their focus. You can simply delete, add, or update these links once a year or so on your own website to keep it current.

Spiritual Take-Away

In the Christian market, this is a key section of your book. A short devotion, Scripture verse, prayer, and parent- or adult-led discussion questions add solid and meaningful content to your published book, even if the story itself doesn't dive deep into spiritual issues.

While you're working on writing your nonfiction manuscript for the Christian market, research ideas for sections you can also include in your back matter. Add several of these to your proposal. You'll be glad you did when it catches an editor's eye. And young readers will be delighted!

Chapter 13

Writing for the Educational Market
Wendy Hinote Lanier

A good way to break into writing for children is to write for the educational market. One of the great things about it is: no writing experience is necessary. Publishers of educational materials are often willing to take a chance on someone who is pre-published, especially if they have experiences or an educational background that makes them an "expert" on a given topic.

Another perk of writing for the educational market is the turnaround time. While it can take years for a traditionally published book to hit the market, educational books are usually published within a few months of their completion. It may be the closest thing there is to instant gratification in the writing world.

And the best part? You get paid. They send a check—with YOUR name on it. That's almost better than getting copies of the book (or magazine article or workbook or whatever) with your name on the cover. Depending on what your bank balance looks like at the time the check arrives, it might be better.

What, Exactly, Do We Mean by "Educational Market"?

So, now that we've established that writing for the educational market might actually be worth your time, we should probably clear up any questions about what we mean by "educational market." Educational publishers are a subset of trade (or traditional) publishers. A closer look at a writer's market guide reveals a section called "classroom" or "educational publishers." This section contains an entire list of publishers who specialize in books and other materials specifically for schools, school libraries, homeschoolers, and other educational settings. This market is also sometimes referred to as the "library book" market.

Projects for the educational market are primarily nonfiction, but there are some fiction opportunities too. The writing is geared to a specific grade level and/or curriculum. And it usually addresses subject matter or skills required by various state education agencies. This includes books that school librarians buy for their school libraries. Students use them to gather information on topics they are learning in the classroom.

Other educational market projects include teachers' guides, textbook supplements, workbooks, teacher resource books, and test items. Most readers are literature-based, but supplementary materials are needed to go with them. Textbooks need workbooks and teacher resources. And test items, while not necessarily easy to write, pay surprisingly well. Opportunities in the educational market abound.

Why Write for the Educational Market?

As we've noted, the educational market can be a good place to start your writing career. While there aren't likely to be any six-figure advances, they do pay. The terms of your agreement with the publisher will spell out exactly what work is expected and how much you will be paid. It's entirely up to you to decide if you want to put in the work for the amount of money they are offering.

For more established writers (which you hope to become), it doesn't hurt to have a mix of income sources. Royalties from traditionally published books are great, but they only come around once (or sometimes twice) a year. Experienced writers will tell you there is value in having more than one kind of writing income.

Writing for the educational market is also good practice in writing tight and working through the editorial process. Having done so shows an editor or agent you have what it takes to carry a project to completion. Better still, following the guidelines and completing a project on time may help you get your foot in the door with one of your own projects down the road.

Be forewarned: projects written for the educational market don't always have your name on the cover. Library books usually do, but other types of educational materials may not. As long as they spell your name correctly on the check, that's all that matters. And they look great on your resumé.

What to Expect

Work for the educational market is usually based on assignment. This type of work is often referred to as "work-for-hire." In this situation, writers are given a set of guidelines, which they are expected to follow. The guidelines include the number of words, number of chapters, target grade level, number and type of sidebars, back matter, etc. Even if you believe your idea for the project is better (and it may well be), this is not the place to try to change their vision or stretch your creative muscles. It's best to follow instructions. To. The. Letter.

At first, finding work in the educational market may require a lot of persistence on your part. Start by finding the type of educational material you want to write. Take note of the publisher. Look for that publisher in your market guide. Do they make assignments? Do they take submissions? Also check their website for submission guidelines.

Be aware that many publishers of educational materials farm out their projects to packagers. They pass along the name and contact information of writers to the companies they work with. This means you may get an email from a name you don't recognize, but the final product will be for a company you contacted.

Be prepared for the fact that you will have very little control over the final product. After a writer finishes a project, there are usually at least two rounds of edits. Once those edits are complete, the project is completely out of the writer's hands. The publisher can, and often does, change things as they deem appropriate. You may or may not agree with the changes, but that's just the nature of this type of work. Don't let it get to you.

And, as far as payment goes, most of the time the payment for an educational project is a flat fee. Royalties are not impossible, but they are rare unless you're creating your own curriculum and selling an entire package.

Basic Tools for the Job

Finally, writing for the educational market can be fun and rewarding. A few tools that can make the job easier include:

- ➤ Children's Writers' Word Book (an absolute MUST)
- ➤ Children's Dictionary (many of your projects are going to require a glossary)
- ➤ Market Guide (see the Educational Publishing section)
- ➤ *Anatomy of Nonfiction* by Margery Facklam and Peggy Thomas (a good resource for writing nonfiction)
- ➤ State Curriculum Guides (see any state's education agency curriculum guides or visit: corestandards.org/the-standards)
- ➤ Word lists (a search for vocabulary lists online should yield grade-level lists)

An Editor's Journey

Deb Haggerty
Publisher
Elk Lake Publishing

What do you love about publishing CRA children's books?

I love the creativity of our writers and illustrators. I also love seeing pictures of children with the books.

What advice can you give to up-and-coming CRA authors?

Children's books in verse seem to sell the best. Remember the illustrations can carry a lot of the ideas you might otherwise put in text.

What types of books are you looking to acquire?

We look for books from preschool through middle grade. We publish all of those except for board books, both fiction and nonfiction.

What are some of your favorite CRA children's (0-18 yrs) books?

I Know What Grandma Does While I'm Napping; The Little Angel Gets a Big Job; Talitha, the Traveling Skirt; all of Max Elliot Anderson's middle-grade books; YA books like the Winter Queen series; *Tranquility*.

What marketing tips can you give to help authors sell more books?

Don't depend on bookstores to sell your books—last year, 75 percent of our books were sold by authors directly; about 23 percent by Amazon, and only 2 percent by bookstores. Find the unusual places to sell your books—craft fairs, schools, libraries, gift shops, community centers.

SECTION 2

Young Children's Books – Board Book to Picture Book

A Writer's Journey
Megan Alms

Author of *Creature from the Woods* (Familius)

Tell us about the experience of getting your first children's book published.

When I first signed with my literary agent, I sent her three picture books I had been working on. She immediately began shopping them around to publishers. Rejection emails started rolling in, but within a couple of months, two publishing houses showed interest in one of my books. The first publisher requested I make edits and send them another draft—but when I returned the edited manuscript, they decided to pass on the project. The second publisher requested a phone call with me. While on the phone, we agreed on a few changes: it would be a board book rather than a picture book, we would remove a few of the pages I'd written, the title would change, and other edits would be made. After another week or so, I signed a contract with them!

Chapter 14

Board Books
Jill Roman Lord

Good Night Moon; *Brown Bear, Brown Bear, What Do You See? Chicka Chicka Boom Boom*. Do these titles sound familiar? Chances are these are board books that you grew up with or that you read to your children. You may still have them in your attic. Board books tend to become favorites of children and parents and may stick around for generations. Let's look at what board books are, what makes them so special, and how to write board books that will maintain long shelf lives.

Board books are crafted with a hard cover and hard pages so kids may truly sink their teeth into them without destroying the books. They are created so babies may turn the pages without tearing them or getting paper cuts. Board books are expensive for publishers to make with the thick pages and colorful art, so they tend to be selective in which ones they accept. They want books that will stick around a while and not flow with the fads of the day. Publishers also love books that make up series. After all, if the readers love one of your books, they will want to read more. So, think in terms of concepts that you may promote as series.

Board books are targeted to newborns to 5-year-olds. There is a big difference between a newborn and 5-year-old, as many 5-year-olds are already beginning to read. So, board books may be broken down further according to ages: 0-2, 2-5. Publishers will vary in the age divisions, but these are the general breakdowns. Please check the publishers' websites for their age breakdowns.

Books for 0-2-year-olds should be less than 250 words and contain 8-16 pages, sometimes up to 24 pages. These will include simple words, simple concepts, and perhaps repetition. Books geared to 2-5-years-olds may have up to 500 words and contain 16-24 pages. My If Jesus series is targeted toward the preschool and up population or 2-5-year-olds. It's a little deep for newborns but works great for this age group. One book in the series is still selling well after more than ten years!

To make your board books special, keep in mind what your targeted age group may be experiencing in their growth and development stages and write from that. For example, the 2-5-year-olds are beginning to learn about God's world, nature, how things are made. They are learning simple Bible stories, who Jesus is, and how to interact with others. They are figuring out new skills, new abilities, how to kick a ball. They are discovering what makes messes, what makes Daddy laugh, and how much Mommy loves them. They are beginning to learn rules of how to obey, how to treat others, how to share. They love to giggle! They adore things that snort, squish, ooze, and go splat. They like to wonder what's on the next page, what's hiding in the corner, and what might pop out. It is so much fun writing for this age group. I try to create stories that include some of these elements in each of my books.

In writing board books, we get to use simple, fun, and creative words, and many, if not all of these books, should include onomatopoeia, which are words that makes sounds like boing, oink, sizzle, boom! We must be selective in our words as we only get to use a few, so pick the best words. Because these books are so short, we should write tightly, introduce the concept on the first page, and make our point quickly. Generally, in board books, we get one point.

And for heaven's sake, let's make our books fun, colorful, joyful, energetic, tender, or entertaining. We want our books to be the ones that the children pick to have read to them. We do this by playing with words until we find the right ones that portray the emotions we want to depict, the sounds we want elicited, and the general mood we hope to create. Our books may certainly have educational value in them as long as the children don't realize they're being educated. They want fun and enjoyable books. The parents will like the educational aspect.

We, as writers of board books, get to introduce children to new concepts or help them dive in deeper. We can show them what it looks like to be nice, to help others, to obey. We can help them explore God's world, witness God's splendor, and experience the love of Jesus. As far as the Christian market, there isn't much that hasn't already been done, so it is up to us as writers to find new twists to old concepts. We get the opportunity to write board books that the youngest children will love and will continue reading on their own as they grow. These are the books that may maintain long shelf lives, may be pulled out of the attic as family favorites, and touch lives for generations to come.

Chapter 15

Thinking in Pictures and Writing Visually
P. K. Hallinan

Yes, you can! You can create as many beautiful children's picture books as you like. All it takes is your willingness to do it! All it takes is your dedication to finish what you start!

Let me explain.

When I was a younger man, I was dissatisfied with my life. I felt like I wasn't contributing anything important to this world. Then one night, I stayed awake for hours—my wife asleep at my side—thinking about what I could do. When morning came, I had made an important decision. I decided to become a novelist.

But God had other plans.

After a month of struggling with writing my first novel, my wife approached and said, "As long as you are trying to become a writer anyway, why don't you write a children's book for our kids for Christmas?" It sounded like a great idea, but there was one problem: I had absolutely no idea how to write—or illustrate—a children's book! So I devised a plan:

I would do it anyway!

I got some colorful paper and a black felt pen and began writing and drawing every evening for the next three weeks. By the time Christmas rolled around, our two sons came downstairs to find *Kenny and Mikey Meet the Jungle People* under the tree. They were very excited! But what pleased me most that day was how much everyone else—neighbors, friends, family, etc.—just raved about it! Was it well written? No. Was it well illustrated? No. Did it offer valuable insights? No.

So … Why was everyone excited about it? Because …

It was fun—and full of love.

Within only weeks, I created a second children's book—*How Really Great to Walk This Way*—and something amazing happened: It was picked up by the very first publisher who read it! Their only concern was that they didn't want to use my art. This was fine with me because I didn't consider myself an artist anyway. But then, eight months later, when the book finally arrived, I discovered just how "flat" professional art could be! My precious story looked more like an arithmetic book than a gift for a child.

And this brought me to another decision.

I decided I would never again allow someone else to do the artwork for one of my books, which meant, of course, I had to learn how to draw! So that's what I did. I began a third book, *The Looking Book*, and worked as hard as I could on every single illustration. But when it was done, I made a sad discovery: My art had improved so much during the illustration process that the whole second half of the book was significantly better illustrated than the first half. This gave me one more decision to make: Do I send it off as it is, or do I go back and re-illustrate the whole first half of the book? The answer should be obvious. I went back and re-illustrated it, believing, even then, that if I did not turn in my best work, I did not deserve to be successful. So, I sent it in, and they published it—using my artwork—and my career as a children's author/illustrator began in earnest! Since then, I have written and illustrated nearly one hundred books for children and have sold more than ten million copies.

And this is where *your* book comes in.

I assume you are reading this chapter because you are interested in creating picture books. Good for you! I wholly encourage you to do this! Children and adults alike love picture books, and you are completely capable of making this happen! Below are some guidelines to help you.

Use Your Own Special Gift

One of the things I love about art is that it is endlessly accommodating of new and different styles. God has given you a unique talent so that you might choose to honor Him with it. If you do this, it's only a matter of time before His light starts shining through your work, and people start embracing your books.

Think in Pictures

I have found it helpful to envision each new page of my upcoming artwork every time I read my manuscript. The key to it, for me, is to focus on scenes that are warm, happy, loving, bright, entertaining, and so forth. In other words, I pour all the goodness and mercy in my heart into my art—and then watch the pictures come to life! So will you!

Keep the Scene Moving

When I wrote *Today is Easter* several years ago, I created a humorous six-page description of an Easter Parade. The problem? The story stalled out because I stayed in the same place too long. So I cut the parade in half. This can be equally true of dialogue. Remember: Nothing is moving when people are talking.

Stay with It

The single most important lesson I have learned about illustrating children's books is this: If I am willing to sit there long enough, drawing and erasing, drawing and erasing, drawing and erasing … Sooner or later, something *usable* will always emerge. And sometimes, something *wonderful* will emerge. I promise.

Be Patient

Finally, back in 1989, I wrote and illustrated a new book, using my sons Ken and Mike as the characters. But no publisher wanted it. So I finally put it on the shelf and attended to other matters. Then, three months later, a publisher called to see if I had any manuscripts available. I said yes and sent them the one on the shelf. Happily, they agreed to publish my book but asked me to re-draw it to clarify who was doing the "speaking" in the pictures. I did this by using only one character. The good news? That same book went on to become *How Do I Love You?* the most successful book of my career, selling more than two million copies over three decades—and still going strong!

> This is why I encourage you to create your book.
> This is why I started with …
> Yes, you can!

Chapter 16

Picture Book Plots
Shannon Anderson

Once upon a time, YOU wanted to write a picture book for kids. You tried to find shortcuts, but there weren't any. You wrote and wrote and sent out your twenty-seventh polished draft but got rejected. You paid someone a lot of money to "fix" your story, but then you didn't even recognize it … or like it anymore.

Then, one day, you decided to check out all of the picture books that you love and study them, really look at how their authors structured their stories. You found writing conferences and invested your time and money to soak up every bit of information you could on the craft of writing. You met some new writing friends that shared your dream and passion for writing and decided to form a trusted critique group to support each other's writing.

You finally developed a story you were proud of. You had the green light from your critique group. You sent it out into the world to carefully selected markets that acquire your genre and style.

You get THE email. Your story has a home. You gasp, reread the email fifty-two times, sing, dance, cry a few happy tears, reread it again and call all of your friends and family with the news.

Can anyone relate to the first paragraph and want to get to the part where your story finally has a home? When you read children's books, the stories can seem so simple. How many times have you enjoyed a picture book and said, "Well, why didn't *I* think of that?"

There are no big secrets to plotting your story, but there are a variety of structures you can follow to ensure that it flows and achieves its purpose. You can opt for different formats, depending on the type of story you want to create.

For young students, you may decide to use a familiar way to organize your book that also teaches something through the type of structure you choose:

- **ABC Books** are a popular way to structure information through a common theme and reinforce the learning of the alphabet. For example, *Shiver Me Letters! A Pirate ABC* by June Sobel.
- **Counting Books** are a technique used to tell a story or share a concept through counting upward or downward. For example, *Ten Black Dots* by Donald Crews. This book teaches counting and also promotes creativity when you see what you can do with your dots.
- **Seasons** in a book can effectively show passage of time and how the changes in seasons affect your characters or nature. For example, *A Tree for All Seasons* by Robin Bernard.

- ➤ **Days of the Week** books offer an opportunity for a short passage of time for a character or event. For example, *Cookie's Week* by Cindy Ward. In this book, an ornery cat gets into trouble almost every day of the week.

- ➤ **Patterns or Repetition** in books can be memorable and fun for kids as they predict what may happen next. For example, *Brown Bear, Brown Bear, What Do You See?* by Eric Carle. Kids read that the Brown Bear sees a Red Bird, then read that the Red Bird sees a Yellow Duck, and so on.

- ➤ **Full Circle Books** are popular and may also follow a pattern. For example, *If you Give a Mouse a Cookie* by Laura Numeroff. Each time the mouse gets something, he asks for something else. By the end of the story, he is asking for a cookie again.

If you are planning to write a more traditional picture book for early readers or to be used as a read-aloud, you may want to try some of these plot structures:

- ➤ **Classic Plot**—the main character(s) has a problem or goal, he/she attempts to solve the problem or attain the goal (usually three times). Just when you think things can't get any worse, the problem is solved, or the goal is met. By the end of the book, the character has changed or grown in some way. An example would be *Princess in Training* by Tammi Sauer.

- ➤ **Parallel Story Plot**—there are two plots unfolding at the same time. It may be two different characters or events. My favorite example is *The Caterpillar and the Polliwog* by Jack Kent. Both the caterpillar and the polliwog are going through a metamorphosis at the same time as the story unfolds.

- ➢ **Cumulative Plot**—there is something that progresses or grows as the story moves on. There is usually a repetitive nature to the book. An example would be, *This is the House that Jack Built* or *My Little Sister Ate One Hare* by Bill Grossman. The author repeats what happens and adds on one more thing each time the cycle continues.
- ➢ **Concept Books**—these books may or may not have a plot, but rather, focus on a certain topic. For example, *Animals in Winter* by Henrietta Bancroft shows what various animals do in the wintertime to survive.
- ➢ **Character Development Books**—these books focus on characters with some kind of social or emotional issue. By the end of the story, the character has faced his/her fear, dealt with jealousy, learned that kindness wins, or some other life lesson. An example of this is *Penelope Perfect* by Shannon Anderson.

There are all kinds of variations to these plot structures and many more techniques out there. Many authors will even combine these formats for a new twist or to fit what they want to accomplish through their stories. Hopefully, this will give you some ways to think about organizing your book. Maybe someday someone will be checking out your books from the library to study the structure you chose! Chances are, someone will enjoy them and say, "Well, why didn't *I* think of that?"

Chapter 17

Rhythm, Rhyme, and Repetition: Mastering the Skill of Writing in Verse
Crystal Bowman

Rhyme has stood the test of time. From Mother Goose and Dr. Seuss to *'Twas the Night Before Christmas*, readers young and old have enjoyed rhyming text for centuries. But as we study publishers' guidelines, we find that many include a firm command: NO RHYME PLEASE!

It's not that publishers don't publish children's books in rhyme; it's that most of what they see just doesn't cut it. It's a waste of their time and energy to sift through the piles of poorly written rhyming text that can ruin a good day at the office. When publishers find a few good writers of rhyme, they stick with those writers rather than take their chances on someone new.

If you have a natural ability for writing in verse—that's great! But you need to master the skill in order to write for publication. Artists, musicians, and athletes have natural abilities, but they work very hard to be skilled at what they do, and writers need to do the same. If you can make it into publishing with exceptional rhyming text, you just might have an ongoing relationship with a publisher!

Rhyming text is most appropriate for board books and picture books. Children are naturally drawn to text with rhythm, rhyme, and metric patterns. As young children listen to their parents read to them, they love to anticipate the rhyming words or say a repetitive word they have learned from the text.

Rhyming Board Books

The rhyming text for board books is often whimsical and playful, incorporating literary devices such as alliteration, repetition, and onomatopoeia. But these elements need to be crafted effectively to avoid creating awkward sentences or impossible tongue twisters. Here's an example that uses these devices correctly:

I walk in the country, what do I see?
A fuzzy, buzzy, bumblebee.
A hoppity toad by the side of the road,
And a big brown cow that moos at me.
MOO, MOO cow,
HOP, HOP toad,
BUZZ, BUZZ fuzzy bumblebee.

In a few short lines, this simple text incorporates rhythm, rhyme, alliteration, onomatopoeia, and repetition. In addition to whimsical wordplay, a board book text may also engage the child by being interactive. In *God's Bright and Beautiful Colors* (Discovery House), each page calls for a response from the child. Here's an example:

ORANGE

The pumpkins in the patch are ORANGE.
ORANGE juice is cool and sweet.
"*Quack, quack, quack*," goes the noisy duck.
Where are the duck's ORANGE feet?

As an adult reads the text, the child will not only be engaged with the rhythm, rhyme, and onomatopoeia but will also search the illustrations to find the duck's orange feet. This is what publishers want.

Rhyming Picture Books

The rhyming text in a picture book takes on more of a story-telling voice rather than wordplay. Once you determine the rhythm, rhyme, and metric pattern, it's important to be consistent throughout the story. A picture book in rhyme will have fewer words than a non-rhyming picture book. While a picture book in prose may have 800-900 words, a picture book in rhyme may have 300-500 words max.

Use strong rhyming words

Words like sad/glad, door/floor, and white/night are exact rhyming words since the vowels and ending consonants sound the same. When the word does not end in a consonant sound such as *sky* and *high*, the vowel sound determines the rhyme. Keep in mind that rhyming words are not always spelled using the same consonants. Words like *sneeze, please, trees,* and *keys* all rhyme because they end with the *eez* sound even though they are spelled differently.

Words like down/around, friend/been, and home/alone are called near rhymes or vowel rhymes because they sound similar but are not exact rhymes with the same ending sound. It's acceptable to use near rhymes now and then but use exact rhymes as often as possible. And by the way—when you make a word plural, it changes the word. *Boy* rhymes with *toy*, but *boys* does not rhyme with *toy*.

When writing in rhyme, always use natural language and write how you talk. Avoid using awkward sentence structure or improper grammar to force a rhyme. Here's an example of a forced rhyme:

"Samantha Sue, get up today!
It's time for school," my mother did say.

Even though *today* and *say* are exact rhymes, the way they are used is unnatural and forced. The following is a better option:

"Samantha Sue, get out of bed.
It's time for school," my mother said.

Master Rhyming Patterns

The most common rhyming pattern for a picture book is a/b/c/b, where the second and fourth lines end with a rhyme, but the first and third do not. Here's an example:

Sam got on the yellow bus,
Sam was new in town.
He didn't know where he should go
or where he should sit down.

With this pattern, the first and third lines are a little longer, using seven or eight beats, while the second and fourth lines use five or six beats.

Another common pattern is a/a/b/b, in which the text is written in couplets. With this pattern, the lines are usually nine, ten, or eleven beats and equal, or nearly equal in length.

This is the house in the middle of town.
Its shutters are crooked and falling down.
The grass is dry, and the weeds are tall.
The flowers don't grow or blossom at all.

Metric Patterns

Metric patterns determine the rhythm of the text and need to be consistent throughout the story. Here are the most commonly used metric patterns for poetry and rhyming stories:

- Iambic ./ *da DUM* (today, tonight, the play)
  Example: My tooth came loose the other day

- Anapest ../ *da da DUM* (overnight, at the park)
  Example: 'Twas the night before Christmas

- Trochee /. *DUM da* (happy, jiffy, take it)
  Example: Children splashing in the ocean

- Dactyl /.. *DUM da da* (happening, anywhere, yes I will)
  Example: Over the river and through the woods
  (Note: A punctuation mark such as a comma or dash can create a pause which counts as a beat and sometimes replaces the need for a word.)

You Can Do It!

As you can see, writing in rhythm and rhyme is far more complex than many writers realize. Writing in rhyme is fun, but fun does not mean easy. And the more you know, the harder it gets! If you are up for the challenge, here are a few more tips:

- Read the best-selling children's books that are written in rhythm and rhyme. Read them over and over and study the rhyme and metric patterns.
- Read the text you've written out loud and have others read it out loud to you.
- Revise. Revise. Revise. Mediocre writing does not get published, but excellent writing does.

Chapter 18

Crafting Holiday Books That Sell
Michelle Medlock Adams

Christmas comes every year. And so does Easter. And so does Thanksgiving. And so does the Fourth of July. Are you seeing a pattern here? Writing holiday books for children is a great way to remain relevant for years to come in both the CRA and ABA markets.

When I first wrote *What Is Easter?* during my lunch hour while working for a Christian magazine back in 2000, I had no idea I'd sell it to Ideals Children's Books (which is now WorthyKids) in 2003. Nor did I have any idea that more than fifteen years later, it'd still be selling twenty thousand copies every single Easter Season, making the ECPA (Evangelical Christian Publishers Association) Juvenile Bestsellers List most every year. In fact, it was in Walmart again this year! Of course, with the success of that little holiday board book, I decided a What Is? series might be a good idea.

It was.

Next came *What Is Christmas?* and then *What Is Thanksgiving?*—both of which are still selling well every year. We tried *What Is Halloween?* but it tanked in the CRA market, so we regrouped and came out with *Trunk or Treat!* a few years later, which was much more Christian-market friendly. However, *What Is Halloween?* came out in a larger format this year and sold very well at Sam's Clubs around the United States. Up next? You guessed it, *What Is America?* debuted in 2019, which will hopefully sell well around Memorial Day, the Fourth of July, President's Day, Veteran's Day, and around election time year after year.

The beauty of writing holiday children's books is two-fold—both the general and Christian markets sell them, and publishers need new holiday picture and board books each year. Here's more good news: many previously successful holiday books will continue selling year after year. In other words, holiday books may only sell seasonally, but they tend to have a long shelf life.

Okay, full disclaimer here. Over the years, I've also written *Memories of the Manger, The Shepherds Shook in Their Shoes, Happy Birthday, Jesus! Sparrow's Easter Song, Little Colt's Palm Sunday, My Funny Valentine,* and *Ha Ha Halloween!* Some of those titles had great runs, though a few of them are now out of print, but others continue selling well every holiday season. And, because I know a good thing when I see one, I have yet another Christmas picture book that just released called, *C Is for Christmas* (Little Lamb Books). I plan to keep on writing holiday children's books as long as there are holidays on the calendar, and I suggest you follow my lead.

But don't just take my word for it. I interviewed several other best-selling CRA authors who have seen their holiday board books and picture books win awards and grace the bookshelves of Barnes & Noble, Target, Walmart, Sam's Club, and more! They all agree that holidays and children's books go hand-in-hand; however, they also agree that crafting a unique Christmas story or finding a different way to tell the Easter Story can be challenging.

Challenging? Yes.

Impossible? No.

Following are some tips and strategies for crafting a marketable holiday children's book from expert authors Crystal Bowman (more than one hundred books for children), Dandi Daley Mackall (over five hundred books for children and adults), and Nancy I. Sanders (over one hundred children's books).

What's your writing process for a holiday children's book?

"The most important thing is coming up with something original because there are so many holiday books in the current market," Bowman says. "So I guess the answer is to start with brainstorming ideas, and then just start writing."

Mackall must narrow down her brainstorming bounty to a single idea before she begins writing.

"I have to start with a single kernel, a theme that I can underscore with rhyme and repetition, or a story that illustrates that theme," explains Mackall. "In *Christmas Blessings* (board book), on each 'turn page,' after rhyming details and images of Christmas, I repeated the line: *Thanks for Christmas blessings!*

"In *One Small Donkey*, the theme was 'Little Ones Can Do Big Things.' It's the story of the first Christmas told in the POV of a little donkey who wishes he were a prancing horse ... until he carries Mary to the stable.

"In *A Shepherd's Christmas*, told through the POV of a shepherd, the takeaway, or theme, is: Jesus could have come to royalty, but he came to us!

"And, in *A Tree For Christmas,* I trace the metaphor of a

tree, from the wood in the manger, to the boat at sea, to the Garden, the crucifixion, and the resurrection."

Sanders starts her process with prayer.

"I ask God to show me what He wants to be taught to children in today's generation and culture for such a time as this about the holy meaning behind a holiday. In other words, I ask God to reveal His heart to me as the writer so I can be His messenger to a lost and hurting world," she shares.

Then comes the brainstorming, according to Sanders.

"This usually begins with researching what the Bible has to say about this holiday and also the historical background and culture and traditions celebrated around the world. I like to then make lists or 'word walls' of words associated with this holiday to help me cover the breadth and depth of this topic, even if it's going to end up as a very simple board book."

Any strategies or tips you can share for those children's writers who long to create a holiday book?

Bowman says it's important to study the market so you'll know what holiday books are already out there.

"What you write has to offer something different and fill a void," she explains. "Once you have your idea and write the text, have it edited by a professional, and be willing to make many revisions. Good writing is not enough--it has to be exceptional."

Mackall agrees with Bowman—you must know the market, and more specifically, you need to know every holiday book the publisher you're submitting to has in recent print.

"They won't want to compete with themselves, right? They may even ask you about the competition to your

Crafting Holiday Books That Sell

proposed book," she adds.

Next?

Mackall suggests the following tips:

- Come up with a unique angle to the holiday.
- Don't rhyme unless you're a perfectionist at meter, rhythm, and rhyme.
- Tell your story in as few words as possible.
- Think about illustrations (but don't supply them—unless you are both an illustrator and writer). "In my first attempt at a Christmas picture book (thirty-five years ago)," she recalls, "the editorial comments pointed out that my first six spreads would all be of one character sitting under a Christmas tree—boring!"
- Even though we usually know the ending to a holiday story, you still need to build suspense.
- In general, stick to one POV, usually a child's.
- Find the emotion in the story and communicate it to the reader.

Sanders agrees with Bowman and Mackall that you need to study the publisher you're submitting to and see what holiday books they've already done, and then look for holes that you could fill in with your stories.

"Don't be discouraged that it's all been done before," she adds. "Just because one publisher may have an alphabet book about Christmas doesn't mean that another one won't want one, too."

An Editor's Journey

Steve Bootsma
Editor
Cadet Quest

What do you love about publishing CRA children's stories?

I love thinking about boys hiding under the bed covers, reading by flashlight, when their parents have said they should be sleeping.

What advice can you give to up-and-coming CRA authors?

If you aren't regularly around children of your target age, find a way to volunteer or interact with children. Don't rely on remembering what it is like to be that age. The world changes rapidly; what a ten-year-old experiences today is not the same as what you experienced as a ten-year-old, or even as the parent of a ten-year-old if that was more than five years ago.

What types of stories are you looking to acquire?

Cadet Quest magazine is geared for boys ages 9-13. I mainly look for short story fiction, although I also use nonfiction articles. Items connected to the theme of each specific issue are preferred. Stories must be wholesome, Christian, and age-appropriate.

What marketing tips can you give to help authors sell more stories?

Be realistic. Don't be cliché. Don't be overly preachy. The real world is messy; things aren't always cleared up by praying once about it, and asking a friend to attend church/Sunday school/boy's club with you doesn't miraculously solve all of his problems. Children can see through the trite and want to be able to relate to the story.

Chapter 19

Interactive Books
Robin Currie

"Then I'll huff, and I'll puff, and I'll blow your house down!" said the Big Bad Wolf.

Did anyone not blooooow along with the wolf?

Children engage with picture books by hearing the words we read aloud (auditory or hearing) and seeing the pictures we show them (visual or sight). There is another sensory opportunity that is often overlooked: touch/action, often called kinesthetic. That's why generations of children know exactly how to blow down pig's houses! Being part of the story experience by blowing the house down makes it memorable.

In any given group, children will have a dominant way of learning: 65 percent visual, 30 percent auditory, and 5 percent kinesthetic. Picture books that appeal to more senses are more engaging and inclusive. Think of *Pat the Bunny*, *The Very Hungry Caterpillar*, and *Where Is Spot?*

Those engage all three ways of learning and are perennial favorites.

Of course, the best stories to remember are those from the Bible. How can we add that kinesthetic dimension to Christian picture books?

Level 1: *Read the story* (all ages). The majority of books require no engagement other than looking at the pictures and no interaction with the reader other than sitting still to listen.

Level 2: *Touch-and-Feel* (birth to 5 years). Very simple board books may feature items attached to the page or holes cut to reveal textures.

Touch the feather.
Feel the woolly coat.
Find the shiny star.

The text may be only one or two words with instructions to enhance the story with a sensory experience. The adults often guide the very young child's hand to experience sensations, perhaps for the first time.

Level 3: *Lift the Flap* (6 months to 3 years). The next level of interacting involves lifting a separate piece of the book to reveal part of the story itself.

What's behind the bush?
Who is making a noise in the tree?

The directions are written into the text of the book, usually in a question form or invitation to lift the flap. The child and adult physically engage in lifting a flap and determine how the figure under the flap relates to the storyline.

Interactive Books

Level 4: *Engage in the text* (6 months to 6 years). The child is invited to make a noise or motion in response to the story.
   Moo like the cow.
   Wiggle fingers for twinkling stars.
   Touch fingertips together for a mountain.
   This is done with directions to the reader within the text itself. These very simple motions bring the child into the words of the story, increasing engagement between reader and listener.

Level 5: *American Sign Language* (3 to 8 years). A much more significant level of interaction is in using American Sign Language to replace certain words in the text; the child actually tells the story with the reader.
   LOVE: *The sign for love is to cross your arms over your chest.*
   This type of book is often enhanced by full descriptions or pictures of the ASL movements as well as pictures for the story. The child assists in actually telling the story, and often the signs afterward are enough to remind the listener of the event or concept.

Level 6: *Retelling* (5 to 12 years). Beyond the book, methods require children old enough to remember without needing to see the pictures.
   This time I'll tell the story, and you make the animals sounds.
   Let's have three volunteers to be Elijah, the wind, and the broom tree.
   If you were one of the magi who just found Jesus, what would you say?
   Directions in the book guide the reader and the listener to act out all or part of the story or tell it in their own words to others. This can happen immediately after reading, or several hours later to increase retention.

Level 7: *Creative Expression* (6 to 12 years). Creative expression expands the story experience in drawing, building, or work with craft materials.

Build Solomon's temple out of blocks.
Draw a mural of creation.
Make the camels out of clay.

The directions can be in the form of endnotes or a sidebar on the page to the adult reader. These activities can be done by any number of children in a home or Sunday school setting.

Which one to use in the story you are writing? In general, the younger the child, the simpler the language, and the more immediate the response has to be. But any story for any age can be more memorable with invitations to kinesthetic response.

So get moving!

SECTION 3

Older Children's Books – Early Readers to YA

A Writer's Journey
Hope Bolinger

A uthor of *Blaze* (Illuminate YA)

Tell us about the experience of getting your first Christian YA book published.

I wrote *Blaze*, a modern-day Daniel, that summer in the span of forty-five days. After having several betas scan through it and conducting it through multiple edits, I pitched it to many editors at a writing conference our school attended.

This was right around the time when the Christian publishers had reached a pivotal point where many wanted books that could reach a general market audience (meaning a modern-day Daniel wouldn't make the cut).

Several pitch sessions in a row of editors telling me, "It won't sell," later, I approached the editor of Lighthouse Publishing of the Carolinas.

He read over my sample, gave me some edits, and told me to submit the book to their YA imprint.

The book made it to the full stage and pub board, but they kept sending back edits. It needed polishing. The characters needed more backstory, writing needed to be enriched with deeper POV, setting needed to be fleshed out.

After a great deal of back and forth, in May 2018, when I'd rolled into my college parking lot after a solemn viewing of *Avengers: Infinity War*, I scrolled through my inbox and found the email from the publisher.

They were going to publish *Blaze*.

Chapter 20

Devotions
Michelle Medlock Adams

If you've ever taken a class about writing devotions, or if you've ever read a daily devotional as part of your quiet time with God, you've probably noticed there's a basic formula or pattern that most devotions follow, no matter if they're written for adults or children.

It usually goes something like this: a scripture, an anecdote/story that leads into the point of the devotional entry, the takeaway, a challenge for the reader, a simple prayer, and often a "thought for the day."

That's pretty standard and fairly easy to duplicate; however, simply following that formula won't guarantee you a publisher, and it won't guarantee that kids will read and love your book.

Here's why.

Because your book of devotions—no matter how well written—will be competing against well-known, best-selling authors and ministers who have had their blockbuster devotional books for adults adapted into children's devotionals, such as: Sarah Young's *Jesus Calling: 365 Devotions for Kids*, Louie Giglio's *Indescribable: 100 Devotions for Kids About God and Science*, and Rick Warren's *The Purpose Driven Life Devotional for Kids,* just to name a few.

How will your devotional book proposal stand out when it reaches an editor's desk?

With a hook.

Hook Your Specific Readership

So, what do I mean by a hook? I mean, your devotional needs to have a specific reader in mind. For example, my forty-day devotional *Get Your Spirit On! Devotions for Cheerleaders* debuted in March 2018 via SonRise Devotionals. That devotional was written for cheerleaders ages 8-12. Seems like a small audience, right? Well, it would appear that way if you didn't know anything about the world of cheerleading, but I knew that specific readership very well. I'd been a cheerleader all through school and even cheered in college; both of my daughters were cheerleaders; I'd served as a cheerleader coach and as a judge at cheer competitions, and I had written many articles for *American Cheerleader* magazine and *Cheer Biz*. And, when my girls were involved in All-Star Cheer, they competed at venues all over the state of Texas, and I encountered thousands of cheerleaders. I knew this group of potential readers was quite large. I just had to prove it in my proposal. So I did a little digging, and I found there were more than 3.6 million cheerleaders over the age of six in the United States at the time.[1] With that statistic and a few more, I got the contract … but not right away.

More than ten publishing houses passed on *Get Your Spirit On! Devotions for Cheerleaders*, commenting they felt it was too niche, too narrow of a market. I'm so thankful SonRise Devotionals decided to take a chance on my cheerleading devotional. With my cheer connections and a solid marketing effort to reach cheer coaches several months in advance of publication, *Get Your Spirit On!* debuted at number one in three different Amazon categories on its launch day.

Kid-Friendly Features

I've always been a bit of a dinosaur nerd. I think it stems from my youngest daughter's obsession with dinosaurs when she was a little girl. We watched every *Land Before Time* movie dozens of times! We couldn't buy her a pet dinosaur, but she settled for a pet lizard named Rocky. She loved all things dino! So it's no wonder why I wrote *Dinosaur Devotions: 75 Dino Discoveries, Bible Truths, Fun Facts, and More!* that debuted with Tommy Nelson in 2018.

To make this devotional even more "dinolicious," I carried that "hook" throughout the book with kid-friendly features that played on the dinosaur theme. As I pointed out in the beginning of this chapter, you'll probably want to include a scripture, an anecdote/story that leads into the point of the devotional entry, the takeaway, a challenge for the reader, a simple prayer, and often a "thought for the day" which is what I did, but I gave them special titles so kids would want to read them. For example, I called

---

[1] "Treating Cheerleading as a Sport," Education Risk Management | Edu Risk Solutions, last modified November 2013, https://www.edurisksolutions.org/Treating-Cheerleading-as-a-Sport/

the scripture "Bible Excavation" and I titled the discussion questions "Digging Deeper" and the writing section "Jurassic Journaling." I also included a special section called "Dinostats" that shared the dinosaur's family, height, length, weight, and diet, and I ended each entry with a "Did You Know?" fact.

When you come up with clever names for the various components of your devotional entry, your readers will know what to expect every time they see those headings. Don't be afraid to think outside the box!

Some Tips for Devo Writing

Write tight: Because devotions are typically short pieces of writing, you'll need to say a lot in only a few words, which tends to be true in every category of children's writing.

Be disciplined in your writing. Cut unnecessary words. Use active verbs. You'll find it's harder to write short than it is to write long … but you'll get better at it! The old joke in the newsroom when I was a reporter was, "I didn't have time to write you a short story, so I wrote you a long one."

Make them fun: Every good piece of writing puts the reader right there, so do that through your opening anecdote. Just because devotions are short pieces of nonfiction writing doesn't mean they should be boring. Be engaging!

Think series: In your proposal, always propose more than one devotional book. For instance, when I wrote the proposal for "Dinosaur Devotions," I also proposed five other devotional books in the series including "Doggie Devotions" which will be published in May 2021. Who knows? You might get a three- or four-book deal!

If you're not sure if you are ready to write a full book of your own devotions, why not start by writing a few entries for a compilation book? Publishing companies like Barbour and Broadstreet often ask for compilation contributors. For example, I was able to write ten devotions in a tween devotional for girls as part of Barbour's "God Hearts Me" series. Reach out to those publishing companies with your writer's CV and samples of your devotional writing and a pitch letter, pitching yourself as a future writer for their devotional compilations.

Devotions are fun to write, and just think: your devotional entry might contain one nugget of truth that could change a child's life forever.

Chapter 21

Biographies
Nancy Lohr

When I was a school librarian, it was common for my young patrons to ask, "Where are your books about real people?" That was code for "Where are your biographies?" Children and teens read biographies for book reports, in connection with other classroom subjects, or simply to learn about "real people"—who they were and what made them important.

A biography is an account of a person's life written by someone other than that person with historically accurate text, written as a well-crafted novel. They can be found in picture book format with minimal text and many illustrations. These books are typically 32 pages long. Middle-grade biographies move into a novel format, have some illustrations, and can range from 64 to 160 pages long. These biographies often feature inventors, statesmen, and people whose character and ingenuity make them interesting to read about. Biographies for tweens and young adults will be print rich with fewer illustrations if any, and they often feature celebrity subjects accomplished in sports or the arts.

Biographies in the Christian market feature biographee who were missionaries, doctors, teachers, hymnwriters, preachers, and more. It is not unusual for the person of note to be a common person serving the Lord with deep resolve and outside of the public spotlight. While general market books may focus on celebrities (enjoyable reads), we should not neglect the quiet success of a steadfast servant of the Lord in stories that can be equally satisfying to read and possibly emulated.

Begin the timeline in the childhood of the biographee so that the reader can easily identify with elements common to every child. The *Childhood of Famous Americans* biographies are helpful books to analyze how this can be done. The arc of the person's life will require the biographee to age as events move chronologically toward the event or reason the person is remembered. The story may end at this high point, but it is not unusual for the biography to continue, ending with a brief summary of the final "chapters" of the person's life.

Develop the timeline based on careful research and then abridge and paraphrase events to result in a concise and compelling account of the larger story.

The plot is dictated by the rise and fall of the actual events, with a conscious effort to avoid a timeline that is flat. (Flatlines in both medicine and children's books are equally deadly.) Much as a novel presents fictional drama appropriate to the target reader, a biography shows the drama of real life—both high adventure and the mundane.

To arrive at historical accuracy, the author needs to research both primary and secondary sources. Primary sources include documented information that originated at the time the biographee lived—sources like diaries, maps, and original artifacts. These sources represent authoritative information from the time of the events, maybe from the biographee himself, but also from others alive at the time. These sources provide the most reliable information possible and may be as close to an interview of a deceased person as possible, but because some of this information resides in private collections or personal memories, some primary sources are difficult to access.

Secondary sources are researched next. These are sources like documents or artifacts derived from primary sources at a later date and include materials like encyclopedias, textbooks, or other biographies. Evaluate this material looking for generalizations, analyses, and interpretations, much as a journalist would evaluate data. The goal is to remove the filters that would color the actual facts of the person's life. Secondary sources are easier to find and have the benefit of offering a perspective of other people from other times, but accuracy and authenticity need to be verified.

Once a timeline has been established and credible information is on hand to flesh out the story, the writing begins. In a biography for children, creative nonfiction will come into play, using fiction-writing techniques to create factually accurate narratives and credible text.

Dialogue is important in a youth biography, but few if any transcripts are available of what the person may have actually said, and so the writer must develop dialogue plausible to what is known of the person, the time, or the situation. Use vocabulary appropriate to the era and the person's station in life. A teacher will sound different from a stevedore. *Oxford English Dictionary* is helpful in establishing the date a word was first used.

Include sensory details that dress your biography in the actual period. Pull the young reader into the biographee's time and place with houses, clothing, foods, and more to add an authentic framework to the story of the person's life. Take care not to reference anything that did not exist at the time the story took place. For example, you cannot allow a character to light a match if the match has not yet been invented.

The author of a biography for Christian children can focus on the image-bearing qualities that are seen in Scripture. Maybe you highlight the inventive, creative thinking that mirrors our Creator and that led to important discoveries or inventions. Perhaps the biographee is a peacemaker or a courageous missionary or one who cares for "the least of these." Look for what is noble in the person and allow that to drive the theme the reader takes away from the biography. This focus is unique to the Christian market and is appreciated by gatekeepers of children in Christian homes, churches, and schools.

Chapter 22

The World of Chapter Books
Dandi Daley Mackall

If writing is your ministry, chapter books offer you a wide-open field ripe for harvest. If you can connect with your readers, who are still forming their worldviews, they may grow up on your books, moving from your preschool easy readers, into your elementary-school early readers, on to your early chapter books, through longer and longer chapter books—until they're all grown up with children of their own. And guess whose books those kids will be reading.

The variety and endless genres and topics that fall into the category of "chapter books" can confuse authors who want to write to this audience. But don't let yourself get overwhelmed. (Don't forget that "God is not a God of confusion, but of peace," 1 Corinthians 14:33).

Keeping in mind that even editors and publishers have differing ideas on the "rules" of chapter books, here are the *general* guidelines:

Easy Readers 100-2,500 words
  Age group: 3-7, preschool and young elementary
  Length: 16, 32, 48, 64 pages, with lots of illustrations
  Vocabulary: low, age-appropriate, sparse; targeting words for beginning readers
  Layout: very short chapters; large print; sentence takes one line
  Subject matter: high interest; can rhyme, or not; child or animal's point of view; fiction, nonfiction, biography, devotionals, anything that interests young readers
  Example: Here are the first three pages of my first easy reader: "Tall girls"/ "Small girls"/ God loves all girls"

My first "I Can Read" easy reader, *Bob the Horse,* didn't rhyme and told a solid story about a very large horse and an equally small horse lover. I wrote *Allyson J. Cat* for my daughters, and it's stayed in print for my granddaughters.

Early Chapter Books
  Age Group: Elementary, ages 6-8
  Length: 48-64 pages generally. Reading levels for this age group can be far apart.
  Subject: Sky's the limit! But the book better be interesting, exciting, fun, engaging.
  Example: *School's First Day of Me!* And my *That's Nat!* series; *A Horse's Best Friend* and *Horse Gentler in Training* from Winnie: The Early Years

Longer Chapter Books
  Age Group: 6-8, 7-10, average 3rd-grade reading level
  Length: 80, 100, 128 pages and longer
  Examples: *Larger-Than-Life Lara; Winnie the Horse Gentler* series; *Just Sayin'; Backyard Horses; Devos for Animal Lovers*

But the best way to determine guidelines for your book is to target a publisher. Pick a line that you believe could be a home for your chapter book. Study books in that line. Count pages and words. Then make your manuscript fit. Imagine the acquisitions editor opening your manuscript and saying to herself, "Hmmm—hope this one is good. It would be a great fit in our line."

Chapter books are naturals for series, though it's good for a beginning writer to offer one book as a stand-alone or as the first book in a series. So what makes a good chapter book series?

Why This? Why You?

You need a unique *hook*, a pitch, an answer to *Why this book?* My first series was *The Cinnamon Lake Mysteries*. Mysteries are great for a series, but it helps to have an extra hook. Mine was nature. The Cinnamon Lakers all loved nature and nature provided the clues to solving the mysteries.

My hook for several of my chapter-book series has been horses. Growing up with horses as my best friends, I learned to connect with them. God allowed me to use my love for horses in *Horsefeathers!*, *Backyard Horses*, *Starlight Animal Rescue,* and *Winnie the Horse Gentler*, which has sold nearly a million copies and continues to be my best seller since 2002. Figure out what God has built into you, what you love, and maybe that's your hook for a series, the answer to *Why you?*

What a Character!

You can't create eight to ten books around an average character. Spend time building your main character and setting her apart from every other character in literature. Live inside her/his head. What does she need, down deep in her heart, where Jesus wants to comfort her? Is he spunky?

A risk-taker? Will you enjoy spending the next couple of years with him? And you'll need a quirky, fascinating band of buddies . . . and villains.

Location, Location, Location!
Your setting will become a character in your series, so be sure to make it intriguing. The night our family drove into Cinnamon Lake to look at a house for sale, I told my husband, "There's a mystery out here." Thankfully, I was right.

Why Not?
What could sink your proposal for a series with a Christian publisher?

Beware of religiosity. We want to celebrate faith and Jesus in our books, but different publishers seek varying degrees of expression. Read at least a dozen chapter books from a publisher before you even think about submitting one. Check out their websites. A good writer can deliver a powerful Christian message without preaching.

Don't give a publisher a reason to reject your manuscript. Join a critique group (Try SCBWI, Society of Children's Book Writers and Illustrators, or a local Christian writer's group.) and listen to their reactions and ideas. Get someone qualified to edit and proofread your manuscript. Rewrite, rewrite, rewrite!

"But my work seems so useless! I have spent my strength for nothing and to no purpose. Yet I leave it all in the Lord's hand; I will trust God for my reward" (Isaiah 49:4 NLT).

Write like it matters . . . because it does.

Chapter 23

Three Keys to Writing Biblical Truth for Children
Christopher Maselli

Most authors don't start writing for children with the hopes of getting rich quick or becoming New York Times bestsellers. They also don't do it because it's "easier than writing for adults" (it's not!). In my experience, most children's authors write because they consider their vocation a *calling*. They have an overall sense of purpose in what they do. They want to share biblical truths with the next generation as a ministry.

Since you're reading this book, this likely rings true for you too. And in today's world, providing children with books featuring a positive, Christian worldview is more important than ever. A study from the Barna Group revealed that "nearly half of all Americans who accept Jesus Christ as their savior do so before reaching the age of 13 (43%), and that two out of three born again Christians

(64%) made that commitment to Christ before their 18th birthday." A mere 23 percent find their faith *after* their twenty-first birthday. The study went on to report, "People who become Christian before their teen years are more likely than those who are converted when older to remain 'absolutely committed' to Christianity."

As authors, our job is critical; we have a hand in helping kids *find* their faith, *understand* their faith, and *enjoy* their faith. Here are three keys to sharing biblical truth with kids in your writing.

Be Bold

Having been a children's author for several decades, I've seen trends come and go in the Christian market. The pendulum swings between a demand for books that are bold in faith and a demand for books that are "seeker-friendly"—that is, clean writing with good morals.

Ultimately, whichever way the market leans, the boldness of your material should be dictated by your *story*. Your characters and plot—not market demand—should drive what happens. That said, knowing what publishers are looking for is still an important consideration in the editing process. Hot trends will always give you an edge but find a balance between what publishers are looking for and what makes your story strong.

Even material that isn't filled with Scripture can be bold. It's about planting seeds. Years ago, I wrote a two-page action comic where the main characters regularly got themselves in jams. In the process, they would shout something like, "God! Please help me!" Time and again, I saw those seeds resonate as children would write to tell me about a jam they got into and how—because of what they saw in the comic—they called out to God for help.

A seed like that may mean more to the reader than you ever could ever imagine—and if it helps one child call on God with the expectation of seeing His deliverance, it more than accomplishes its goal.

Don't Be Preachy

Beware: There's a fine line between being *bold* and being *preachy*. No reader—and certainly no editor—wants a book that reads as though it's trying to tell them how to live.

Never, ever talk down to kids. They recognize when you do. Even at a young age, children know the difference between listening to a teacher and talking to a friend. When you're writing, you're their friend *first*. You're sharing a story, igniting their imagination, allowing your material to sow the seed.

Furthermore, when you write a story, allow the young characters in the story to solve their problems themselves. Don't allow a parent or other adult to step in and save the day. Let the reader see how your characters use what they learn from life and from the Bible to overcome their challenges.

One way to get in the flow of talking *with* kids instead of *at* them is to … well … talk with kids! I purposely spend time engaging with kids in my target audience when writing a book to be sure I stay "on their level." It's as simple as volunteering at a youth group or school. Doing so will fuel your writing to reach children and teens where they're at, leaving misconceptions at the door.

Be Real

Finally, be real. This can be difficult since we live in a society that values only putting our best image forward on social media—and even at church. But kids, especially teenagers, thrive on reality and honesty. Your story can still take place in a fantastic setting—a sci-fi world, a fantasy realm, or even a metropolis of superheroes. But the characters in those amazing worlds should display down-to-earth, real emotions and deal with struggles of the human condition.

If your characters face a tough time or make a mistake, don't be afraid to let them show it—then reveal how they must deal with the consequences of their actions. So long as the grit is authentic, you'll be surprised how well kids can handle the truth. (Of course, topics should always be age-appropriate.)

This also means you don't have to hold back when it comes to the reality of living by faith. When suitable, allow your characters, within the confines of *who they are,* to be proactive with their faith. Too many characters in Christian literature are *reactive*—authors create protagonists who simply try to "hold on" when trouble hits. But kids need to understand that faith is *proactive* too. In other words, what does it mean to live a Christian life in today's world, day by day by day? Kids love discovering how to navigate the "every day" maze and live a life of adventure in God.

When you share your faith in a bold, non-preachy, yet honest way, your readers will not only enjoy your story, but they'll receive the seeds of biblical truth that they can count on for the rest of their lives.

Amy Houts

Author of more than seventy books for young children including, *God's Protection Covers Me* (Beaming Books). She has authored sixty picture books for the Compass Publishing series titled Compass Children's Classics, writing EFL (English as a Foreign Language) books for early grades on assignment. It's a joy for Amy to share Bible truths and God's love with young children through her writing. Amy and her husband, Steve, are the parents of two grown daughters and have three grandchildren.

What advice can you give to first-time authors?

Develop a friendship with a Christian author who understands your heart. Their support, encouragement, and prayer are exactly what you will need in your writing journey.

Do you have any nuggets of wisdom you can share about writing Christian children's books?

Learn everything you can about writing well either through courses, workshops, and/or conferences. I've been published for over thirty years, and I am still learning and growing as a writer. It's easier than ever now with webinars and online courses.

What has been your greatest struggle in your publishing journey?

Rejection. It's hard not to despair. I think about what my friend, author Mindy Baker, said, "I am trusting that God has me on this path for a reason and believing that He will open up the next thing for me in His time."

Chapter 24

Writing for Middle Grade
Tim Shoemaker

Tough ... but rewarding. Those three words describe what it's like to write for middle-grade readers. And writing for this market is critically important—if you want to impact generations to come. This market has often been underrated, but our middle-grade students represent the future.

Think about middle-graders. They're in a rough spot—stuck between being a kid and growing up too fast. So many at this age become addicted to pornography—and their phones. They're short on integrity—and long on compromise. They're bored with church—and the Bible.

Reaching this market is doable, but we must write well. Here are some tips and suggestions to help us do exactly that.

Seven Gotta Haves

There are important things our book needs—if we're going to get a middle-grade student to read it. Some of these are obvious—but they still need to be said.

1. **Great Cover.** This is the first thing a middle-grader will look at. Sure, if we publish traditionally, the publisher makes the cover decisions—not the author. But the tactful author has *some* input. And if we self-publish, we must pay for a *good* cover. Remember, middle-grade students want to "read up." They want to appear older than they are. Avoiding a cover that looks too juvenile is smart.
2. **White Space.** The second thing a reader will check is the amount of white space on the pages. If we have page after page of margin-to-margin copy, likely they'll pass right by our book. Dialogue and interior thoughts break up the page nicely. And it's a really good idea to keep our chapters short. Often a reader will flip through the book to see how long the chapters are before making the reading decision.
3. **Powerful Opening.** "A weak opening line greets us like a limp handshake." I don't know who first said that—but it's true. Our opening lines must intrigue readers—or hint at trouble. We can start with a one-liner that grabs the reader—or maybe use hyperbole.
4. **Action.** Middle-grade readers need something happening—or about to happen if we're going to hold their attention for long. So we limit the narration and description—and resist the urge to summarize action instead of showing it in real time.

5. **Show the Story.** Our readers are used to *watching* stories on screens. As we write, we don't want to *tell* readers a story ... we want to *show* it. Sure, there are places where "telling" the story is fine ... when transitioning between scenes or spanning great lengths of time, etc. But then let's get right back to showing. Our readers want to experience the story.
6. **Deep Point of View.** Often the more dedicated we are to stay in our protagonist's head, the easier our readers identify with that character. That bonds them to our book. Here are some things we can consider about our character in every scene. What is our character's perspective on life ... how do they see things? What is our character's personality ... how would it play out in this scene? What is our character's priority ... what is it they want—and how does that influence them right now? What is your character's predisposition ... what kind of mood are they in at the moment? If we keep these in mind, we'll write in a deeper POV.
7. **Believability.** What our character does. Says. Every aspect of our story needs to be believable. Possible. Probable. If the reader questions the plausibility of something in our book, we'll rip them out of the story experience. We don't want that to happen. A story that comes across as unbelievable often simply entertains—and loses its ability to inspire readers deeply.

One Cheap Shot to Avoid

Writers for middle grade often make parents, teachers, and people in authority look dumb. That's often a cheap shot. It's stereotypical, lazy writing. While it can be highly entertaining, let's consider the outcome. Middle graders don't talk to their parents enough as it is—and this kind of writing can reinforce that behavior. With good writing—where protagonists can find real help and encouragement from adults—we encourage readers to seek out responsible adults for wisdom and direction in real life.

Two Ways to Shoot Higher

1. **Keep It Clean.** Often Christian writers struggle with how much language or sex to use ... even when writing for middle grade. The truth is, we don't need either to make our writing more "real" or appealing. A great story—written well—with likeable characters is all we need.
2. **Keep It Real.** Often Christian fiction can be downright hokey. Stories are predictable—or seem agenda-driven. Often a character recounting a sermon—or even a salvation scene can seem forced. We do well to study how Jesus taught. He was all about conveying truth. So let's give our readers truth—and trust that the truth will lead them to God.

Two Secrets That Make All the Difference

1. **Think of Middle-Grade Readers as Smart.** They're as smart as we are—or more—in technology ... and often math. If we think of them as just "kids" ... likely we'll write down to them, repeat ourselves to make sure readers get our point, or our writing will take on a "parental" tone. Readers won't like that.
2. **Think of Middle-Grade Readers as Lacking Experience.** This is the issue. They're smart, but they lack the experience and tools to cope with life. They lack wisdom. How can we help them? Convey

wisdom to our readers through the experiences of our characters.

Writing for middle-grade readers. It's a chance to help kids in a difficult time of life. A chance to give them wisdom and truth ... to influence them so they don't become broken adults. Write well ... and likely your story will impact readers in the CRA and ABA market. Yes, it's tough ... but so incredibly rewarding.

Chapter 25

Writing Craft Books
Karen Whiting

Crafts provide fun for children while helping them develop small motor coordination. When I wrote my God's Girls books that combine faith and crafts, I had no idea the books would have twenty printings. That shows the popularity of such books. My craft-related books include puppetry books and general crafts for girls. I also add crafts to other books, such as a few crafts in devotional books for boys and craft ideas in some of the daily devotions for young girls.

I started with selling puppet and craft ideas to magazines and Sunday school take-home papers. As a child, I enjoyed making things and learning all sorts of needlework skills. That made it easy for me to come up with ideas for my books. As a Christian, I like to connect crafts to biblical principles. Using hands while learning helps children remember the concepts. For example, a devotion on Mary, the mother of Jesus, spoke about family ties, so I paired it with a craft on making a macramé belt. This way, girls could wear the belt and think about Mary and Jesus. They also learned a skill of using knots to make something.

I like to inspire a child's imagination, and crafts make a great vehicle for doing that. Once a child makes a craft, I suggest they make another and add their own design. So, with a macramé belt, I can suggest they make another one using two or more colors of macramé cord or add beads onto the strands of cord for pops of color.

What's a Good Process for Writing a Craft Book?

First, choose the medium or book concept. I chose felt and paper puppets (medium is felt and paper plus topic is puppets) for one book and women in the Bible for the God's Girls books and focused on a virtue for each woman as my concept. For an upcoming book, I chose paper as the medium.

Be sure the crafts are age-appropriate and affordable. Parents prefer children to use simple and inexpensive materials. Experiment and let children try making them. I had focus groups of children the age of the readers come to my home to make the crafts. Other times I set up a craft table at an event or a store. This makes sure the crafts are kid-tested. It's also a good way to check that your directions are clearly stated and that any patterns are correct.

Patterns, supply lists, and directions take up more space with less words. Keep that in mind when you consider the length of the book and how many projects to include. Take photos as you create the crafts. If the publisher cannot afford color art, the photos can be displayed on a Pinterest board with a link in the book to the board.

Carefully write the supply and tool list as well as the directions. I write the list as I gather my supplies and start to make a craft. I pause after each step to write the directions for that step. Then I wait a week or more before I take the list and remake the craft. I want to be sure I can duplicate it from the list and the directions. That way I catch any missing step or supply.

Coordinating Concept with Crafts

When I design a book that will combine faith and crafts, I make lists of possible crafts for the age of the reader and also faith concepts I hope to share. So, for *God's Girls*, I listed thirty women in the Bible and a virtue related to each one. I also listed more than thirty crafts and matched the crafts to the virtues. I usually create a spreadsheet where each row contains the craft, concept, and supplies used.

For puppets, I added ideas of puppet shows to do with each character created. I also added pages on how to manipulate the puppets and how to create a puppet show. I usually include characteristics of the specific puppet plus biblical themes that go with it. So a pig puppet is talked about in several scriptures (don't cast pearls at swine, the prodigal son, and others). A pig is known to wallow in the mud and eat most anything. From those ideas, I write prompts for using the puppet in a show.

Once they make several puppets in a book, they have the skills to create their own puppets, such as a favorite animal not covered in the book. You can suggest they check animal pictures in coloring books or online images to create the head shapes and faces as they make their own puppet patterns.

Putting the Book Together

The opening of the book should share enthusiasm for the craft and ideas of how the crafts can be used. Then list all the basic supplies used in the book so children can gather them into a container.

Have a few pages that explain the supplies, such as different types of adhesives and safety issues with each.

Include a disclaimer as you can never cover all the unusual and unsafe ways a child might use a supply or tool. Include a safety note for parents to supervise the craft making and go over safety with the child.

Then organize categories. It might be by the type of medium like paper or yarn crafts in separate chapters. Or it might be by the type of crafts like crafts to wear, crafts to decorate your room, or crafts that make good gifts.

Decide the approach of sharing the concept and the craft. For God's Girls, I start each chapter with a devotion on women in the Bible followed by journal prompts to help girls think about the virtue of the women studied. This is followed by the craft instructions. At the end of each chapter, I have a few ideas of how to add their own creativity to the craft. The patterns are with the craft. In a different book, the patterns are in the back of the book in an appendix.

Studying the Market

Check out various craft books and study the layout of concepts, crafts, directions, and supply lists. That helps you decide how to approach your own craft books. Also, check out Pinterest to see what's there and how your book will stand out from what people can find online. The crafts online are usually not paired with faith concepts or even ways to use the craft.

Visit craft stores regularly to discover new materials. For me, walking through a craft store, I can quickly come up with ideas of things to make. I buy new materials to play with them and see what I can do with such supplies.

Craft books are easy to market with Pinterest, Instagram, and Facebook Live, where you can easily display crafts and demonstrate how to make them.

Turn your hobby or childhood craft memories into a book. You'll have fun while creating a sellable product!

Chapter 26

Writing Nonfiction for YA
Bethany Jett

We are not the cool kids.

By the time a trend has reached adult ears, it's been long gone, dead and buried, and the only thing left to do is whisper YOLO at the embarrassment we've caused ourselves and admit that we are part of the "Okay, Boomer" problem even if we're not Baby Boomers at all.

Got that, Karen?

Writing for the YA audience is a delicate balance of sharing a truth and blending it with the story in a way that's relatable to what they're going through without lacing the message with too-specific details that date the author and alienate the reader, despite the cyclical nature of life. After all, the 1980s dorky bookworm is today's VSCO girl.

Sksksksksksk.

Some truths are self-evident, to quote the Declaration of Independence, and those truths are the underlying issues that YA authors are trying to uncover.

Let's take dating, for example. A one-night hook-up is as easy as scrolling through photos and swiping right … at least until the next big thing comes along. But the underlying truth is that people are lonely, searching for connection, and are willing to trade their bodies in hopes of intimacy.

Particularly with nonfiction, YA authors have to pinpoint that underlying truth and be able to address the culture without condemnation so the reader can move along the path to self-help, Christian living, or whatever goal the author is trying to accomplish.

The truth is, young adults are more adult than this same age demographic was even five or ten years ago. Instant access to every type of debauchery has made our kids grow up faster than perhaps we wish, but with their youth comes a naiveté simply because they don't have the life experience.

But talking down to a YA audience is one of the biggest mistakes an author can make. The assumption is that the reader understands the adult nature of relationships, so the challenge is to present those situations in a manner relatable to readers who may not have graduated from high school, college, or have ever had to support themselves.

The underlying truths, the core messaging, is the key. Sometimes YA readers are taking on adult responsibilities, like caring for their siblings or working multiple jobs to help the family make ends meet. Sometimes they understand what it's like not to know where their next meal is coming from. And sadly, because of their age, they are often not in a position to change their circumstances.

Hence, the beauty and brilliance of books and the absolute privilege it is to write for a YA audience. We provide escapism, a lifeline, a world where they can identify as a character or from our own experiences and, throughout the stories, find their own way out of their real-life situations. As authors, we don't shy away from the hard scenes or the difficult and awkward topics.

We dive straight in, sharing the lessons in a way that helps the readers feel as though they are not alone. We give words to their feelings and a voice to their thoughts. Most appropriately, we seek to help them untangle their own thought processes and come to conclusions on their own.

We offer hope.

The vast majority of those who attempt to write for the YA audience do so intending to pass on teachable moments—a noble objective—but the writing becomes stilted, cliché, or the inevitable: pages full of slang, acronyms, or out-of-date references that turn off the reader.

My first editor left strong red circles all over the pages of my first YA nonfiction manuscript. "This would sound great if you said it from the stage," he wrote. "But in print, it's too strong and preachy."

Message received.

The skill of YA is to come alongside the reader. For nonfiction, picture the two of you sitting next to each other in a coffee shop, swapping stories, drinking overpriced-but-delicious Frappuccinos with caramel drizzle. There is a mentorship. Relationship. Connection. Value. The lessons are firm but softened with self-deprecation and illustration. There's a light at the end of the tunnel.

For fiction, you're taking the reader on a journey of internal exploration as they read through your stories. They are the characters, and your characters are them. There is identification. Realization. A desire to be understood and to come out stronger on the other end of The End.

Writing for YA is a gift, and one to be mastered with the respect it deserves. You've been chosen, not because you're the cool kid, but you're the writer who makes your readers feel as if *they are*.

An Editor's Journey

Karissa Taylor
Editor
Thomas Nelson/Harper Collins Christian Publishing

What do you love about publishing CRA children's books?

A great children's book has a message that's simple enough for kids to understand but strong enough to affect any heart at any age. God-focused children's books can illuminate who God is in a simple yet profoundly deep way. When children read these books, they build a relationship with God, and they trust what they learn about Him. It's an honor to share these truths with those who are discovering them for the first time, and the hope is that they will store them in their hearts for years to come.

What are some of your favorite CRA children's (0-18 yrs) books?

Children don't always understand the connection between God and science. Often, they see schoolteachers teaching about science and Sunday school teachers teaching about God, and the two don't always mix. But science is an expression of God's power, majesty, and brilliance, and Louie Giglio makes that clear in his two children's devotionals, *Indescribable* and *How Great Is Our God*. In these books, kids can learn about the effects of weather, the wonders of our amazing bodies, some surprising animal facts, and the mysteries of the universe, and they discover how great and indescribable our God truly is. *God, I Know You're There* is magical. It's not an easy feat to combine beautiful and meaningful words with the perfect illustrations to bring those words to life, but that's exactly what happened with this book. Bonnie Rickner Jensen made a difficult concept—God's presence—something that little ones can grasp, and Lucy Fleming's artwork is simply stunning and truly shows the wonder of God's creation. *Only You Can Be You* combines the adventure of childhood, the wonder of the imagination, and the celebration of being exactly who God made us to be. This picture book shows kids that what makes them different is what makes them great—both encouraging children to embrace their differences while also appreciate the differences they see in others. This is the perfect age to help children realize that people aren't going to be the same, and that's okay—in fact, it's great!

Chapter 27

Writing YA That Sells in the Christian Market
Caroline George

Young adult fiction is like the TikTok app—designed for teenagers but enjoyed by people of all ages. No other genre offers the same level of flexibility, diverse readership, and community-mindedness. That said, YA writers must understand the genre and market, so they know how to capture a publisher's attention.

I never expected to write YA fiction for the Christian market. When I released my first book at age fifteen, I planned to build a career in the general market. However, a series of God-planned events guided me into the Christian publishing industry. I worked for HarperCollins Christian and Hillsong Church before I signed a three-book deal with Thomas Nelson.

Writing for the Christian market is a dream come true, but the journey from writer to author included a rollercoaster of learning curves. In this chapter, I'll share the dos and don'ts of writing YA for the CRA. I will also give insight into market changes and platform growth.

The CRA and ABA look for similar elements when acquiring YA titles. Regardless of your author goals, the following information will help you take your next publishing steps.

Changes within the CRA Publishing Landscape

The CRA fiction market has changed over the past few years. Its YA releases have shifted from blatant Christian titles to clean, faith-based projects geared toward secular readers. More and more CRA publishers are acquiring YA books with cross-market appeal to increase sales—and to share Christian messages with a broader audience.

CRA publishers also put an emphasis on author platform, especially when seeking nonfiction and YA projects. They expect authors to know their target audience (their potential readership), engage with that audience, and work to sell their books.

Don't be alarmed if you have a small platform or wrote a YA novel that doesn't cater to cross-market readership. Many small presses acquire niche titles, meaning they're more accepting of projects geared toward specific audiences.

The Purpose of Platform and Why It's Needed

I teach branding and social media workshops at conferences across the country. During each session, I watch attendees go from interested to skeptical to downright frustrated. They ask me, "How many followers do I need to land a book deal? Why should I spend time on social media when I could use that time to write? Aren't publishers responsible for marketing books?"

When I attended my first writing conference, I asked similar questions. I hated the thought of developing my social media presence and author brand. Now over eight years into my author journey, I see the value of platform and understand its purpose.

The harsh reality: If an author wants to succeed in the YA genre, they need platform. I will explain why in a moment, but first, let's define the "frenemy" known as platform.

Platform refers to someone's realm of influence—who they know and how that audience translates into book sales. Platform includes social media, speaking engagements, newsletter subscribers, organizational memberships, etc.

Social media algorithms change every few months, so follower count doesn't always determine a platform's value. For example, if someone has an Instagram with five hundred loyal followers who are likely to purchase the person's book, then that platform would be more valuable than someone's non-writer-related Facebook page with five thousand likes.

Platform value is determined by the question: Will the audience buy the book?

My publishing motto is 'Books are accessories to their messages.' Nowadays, authors and publishers work to sell the complete reader experience—the book, the author, the online community. Take Instagram, for example. YA readers communicate with each other via hashtags like #Bookstagram. They chat about their favorite reads and engage with authors.

CRA and ABA publishers want to work with platform-savvy authors, not because they want to avoid marketing responsibilities, but because they know author-reader connections sell books. Genuine relationships surpass promotional endeavors.

Writers, we do the business so we can tell the stories. We don't have to love platform. We just need to love our writing enough to advocate for it through platform.

The Dos and Don'ts of Writing YA for the Christian Market

Although cross-market appeal and platform are needed to sell YA in the CRA, content plays a huge role in enticing both publishers and readers. A YA title must have a clearly defined subgenre, a genre-appropriate word count, and recent comparable titles. The book also needs a strong hook. In publishing, acquisition editors look for "same but different," meaning they want books that cater to an established readership but are unique enough to capture attention.

Do: Create a "same but different" concept with a clearly defined readership.

Don't: Write a cliché story that violates genre guidelines.

Young adult literature emphasizes character voice, which is one reason why the genre interests so many readers. One mistake I see a lot of writers—especially mature writers—make: They attempt to mimic a teen voice without doing research. The product tends to sound outdated and cheesy, sometimes "preachy" if the writer hopes to publish in CRA.

Do: Study YA books to get a feel for the voice and style, then practice writing as different characters.

Don't: Attempt to mimic a teen voice without reading in the YA genre.

Overall, selling YA in the Christian market is almost identical to selling YA in the ABA but with the bonus of working with Jesus-followers. Some tips to boost chances of publication:

- Enter writing contests. Awards add credibility to a proposal.
- Keep writing. Practice, practice, practice. I'm a firm believer that if a writer stays in the business long enough, they will experience success.
- Enlist the help of beta readers. Find people with a knowledge of YA fiction and ask them to critique your work.
- Be open to collaborations. Many CRA publishers now have a partnership mindset. They want long-term relationships with authors. That said, authors who are easygoing and willing to make alterations will land multi-book contracts.

Chapter 28

Writing YA Fiction: What Teens Really Want to Hear and What They Don't

Tessa Hall

I had an ambitious goal as a fifteen-year-old—and that was to write a contemporary YA fiction book. Not just any book. I wanted to write a story that could whet the young reader's appetite for a relationship with Christ yet remain authentic to the teen culture as well.

You see, I had noticed a lack of books that filled this void. I was often repulsed by the content presented in YA fiction contemporary books. These books, which were published in the general market, may have done an accurate job of reflecting the teen culture—but these authors presented issues, such as teenage drinking, in a way that seemed to *promote* them.

However, I noticed the opposite problem in the Christian market: Some YA Christian fiction authors tried to veer as far away from promoting this kind of behavior as possible; yet, in doing so, their stories often came across as cheesy. Unrealistic. Preachy.

Where were the books that reflected everyday teen issues accurately, while weaving in spiritual truths as well? The books that could offer escapism and entertain teens while presenting *clean* content instead?

Over the past several years, I have witnessed an unfortunate decline in the Christian YA market. The general YA fiction market, though, seems to be booming now more than ever. I believe this is because most YA fiction authors in the general market understand teens. Shouldn't we Christians learn to do the same?

I believe we can make a comeback in this genre. There is power in storytelling.

But first, we must learn to strike the balancing act of writing inspirational stories while remaining authentic to the teen culture today. We can do this by being familiar with our target audience—understanding why they read and how we can write a book that appeals to their interests while avoiding the temptation to preach.

We Must Understand Teenagers

The YA writers who are out of touch with today's teen culture seem to simply rely on their own experiences as teenagers to reach this audience. The problem with this? The teen culture is in a constant state of motion. Teenagers are smart and trust me, they can discern if an author is writing the book for *yesterday's* teen culture rather than today's.

So since we are authors for teens, let us make it a priority to stay in touch with them. We can do this by hanging out with them, striking conversations with them, getting involved in youth ministry, and even connecting with teen readers online. (In a non-creepy way, of course.)

We Must Understand Why Teenagers Read

Why do teenagers read, and what do they search for in these stories? It may be easier to answer these questions once we first consider the stories they are *not* interested in reading.

The average teen reader is not likely to finish reading a book that preaches at them. Think about it: Teens often read so they can *escape* the lessons and commands they're surrounded by in school and home.

We should also be aware of the slang terminology used in our books. When we include slang terminology of *yesteryear*, we risk popping the bubble of the fictive dream experience we wish to create.

Now, what is it that teens do look for in stories?

1. Escapism
2. Connection
3. The opportunity to understand, learn, and explore

Reading allows teenagers to broaden their horizons and think for themselves. It provides them with a sense of belonging when they read about characters of which they can identify. Yet, they will also read books to explore unfamiliar issues or topics they wish to understand. YA books offer insight on diverse characters, settings, topics, and time periods. These stories offer teens a sense of escapism and adventure that they may not otherwise have the privilege of enjoying in real life.

Overall, these books offer a sense of companionship. When we understand this, we can then write books that speak *to* them (like a friend would) rather than books that speak *at* them (like a preacher or teacher would).

We Must Understand How to Avoid Preaching

As a Christian fiction author, is it possible to weave in spiritual truths without preaching? I believe so.

It comes down to the good ol' advice to *show* instead of *tell*.

In the New Testament, when Jesus wanted to communicate lessons, what method did He use? Storytelling. He didn't hit the disciples over the head with these lessons; rather, these lessons were grasped through the vehicle of a story.

We, too, can allow our stories to do the talking. Our books' spiritual thread can be illustrated through our main character's transformation.

The journey our main characters take should allow for character growth. They should be different at the end of the story than they were at the beginning. (Not *perfect*, but *different*.) Thus, the theme of the book is delivered.

In a more practical sense, how can you discern if you're preaching? Ask yourself: Am I trying to drive a point home? Am I using a character as a means to teach the reader a lesson? Is my story filled with Scriptures, Christian terminology, and characters listening to sermons? If so, the readers will probably consider the book to be preachy.

In case you were wondering—that book I began writing at fifteen years old? It was published four years later. Even today I receive letters from teens who tell me how the book, *Purple Moon*, inspired them to live for Christ. This is evidence that, yes, it is possible to write authentic yet inspirational stories for teens.

My prayer is that you will not become discouraged by the state of the Christian YA market today. Instead, may you follow God's leading by writing the story He has placed on your heart—all the while following the principles laid out in this chapter. Trust that, through the words you pen, God can do the work within the hearts of your recipients.

It is only by writing books teens enjoy will we begin to see a comeback in this market. We will see teens devouring books that speak to them without preaching. Books that portray realism without promoting bad morals.

Just like the kind of books I searched for when I was a teen.

Alyssa Roat

A literary agent with Cyle Young Literary Elite, Alyssa Roat is a professional writing major at Taylor University, the online editor for *The Echo News*, a freelance editor with Sherpa Editing Services, and a research assistant at Zondervan Library. She has also worked for Illuminate YA Publishing and Little Lamb Books. Dozens of her articles have been featured in various publications, and she has won several awards, including second place in the Jerry B. Jenkins short story contest, first place in the 2016 We the Students Essay Contest out of twenty thousand entrants, and first place in the 2018 Friends of Falun Gong college division poetry contest. She can be found at www.alyssawrote.wordpress.com.

Do you have any nuggets of wisdom you can share about writing Christian children's books?

In middle-grade/YA fiction, my passion is reaching kids and teens both who are raised in Christian households and those who might know nothing about Jesus. There's a lot of junk out there, and I want to give them an alternative. Thus, my books might not overtly say a ton about God or religion at all. However, for the books that are specifically for a Christian audience, I would say it's important to remember not to bash your readers over the head with the Bible. Tell a good story first. Show how God works in your characters' lives (and not by miraculously solving all their problems; that's not how life works). Kids are smarter than that. If all we give them are squeaky clean, trite answers, they're going to look elsewhere for answers. We have such a wonderful opportunity to both entertain and edify.

What has been your greatest joy in your publishing journey?

The writing process is what I love: coming up with the story, meeting the characters, going along for the ride. The second best is probably when other people love the story as well.

What has been your greatest struggle in your publishing journey?

Patience. There is a lot of waiting, a lot of self-doubt, a lot of agonizing. You can always get better, so always work to improve your craft, but also don't get discouraged and think you're a terrible, awful writer and quit just because one agent/publisher/editor didn't like your manuscript. These things take time. But it's worth it.

SECTION 4

Selling Children's Books

A Writer's Journey
Debbie Spence

Author of *Broken Crayons Color Too* (Little Lamb)

Tell us about the experience of getting your first Christian children's book published.

After waiting for years, it was time. My children, and homeschooling for twenty-four years, had been my focus, but now it was my turn to pursue my dreams. I began by scheduling a one-hour strategy appointment with Platinum Literary Agency. Michelle Medlock Adams and Bethany Jett both helped me with a plan during our Zoom call. They gave me ideas and suggestions. They offered me a discount to attend the North Carolina Christian Writers Conference. I signed up and began to prepare. I signed up for a live pre-conference critique with Cyle Young. He critiqued my book and gave me suggestions on how to increase my platform. I signed up for Serious Writer Academy and took numerous classes to learn how to prepare for the conference. I took Cyle's suggestions and worked on my book. I learned from the online classes that I needed to have five to seven finished projects to pitch at the conference. I buckled down and wrote more books.

I worked with an editor so that they would be in good shape for the conference. I used an e-book that I had already completed and offered it on Book Funnel and increased by subscribers by three hundred before the conference. I did my research on the editors and publishers that would be attending the conference. I wanted my appointments to matter and be a good fit for those I hoped to connect with. Once at the conference, I felt like I was there for my final exam, but I knew I had prepared and that I had done my homework. Cyle was my first appointment. He liked my edits and improvements and was impressed with my increased subscriber numbers, but they still were not high enough. I needed a larger platform. He told me that I was a good writer, and I should talk to his junior agents. This encouraged me. My next appointment was with Little Lamb Books. She read my stories, pulled one out, and said, "I want this." She told me to find an agent and tell them that she wants one of my stories, so they should represent me. (It was not my original book.) I was so excited and shocked that I almost missed my next appointment. I ran to my next appointment late, breathless and full of joy. She became my agent. Everything fell into place at the conference, but preparation was the key.

Chapter 29

Platform
Cyle Young

Platform is King. But what exactly is it?

Platform is the term used to describe your discoverability in a crowded world of seven billion people. Essentially, it's a combination of factors that help an agent or editor determine how large of a following you have, and how easy it will be for readers to find you and your books. The easier you are to find, the larger your platform.

There is no exact science to platform, and most people just know it when they see it. Clear as mud?

I will try to help you quantify and qualify your platform so you can share it to potential agents and publishers. Platform used to be as simple as having a large social media following, such as a hundred thousand Twitter followers or ten thousand newsletter subscribers. But over the years, it has become a much more complex and convoluted system of subjective determinations.

There are things that still are definitely platform, but they usually include five or six zeroes, such as eighty thousand Instagram followers, or five million monthly hits on your website. Those kind of metrics will always get someone's attention.

Most authors don't have the platform needed to work with some of the largest publishers. But don't be forlorn, remember platform is subjective, and different size publishers require different levels or types of platform. Some mid-size and independent publishers will be excited about thousands of social media followers and hundreds of email subscribers. A publisher's average book sales generally determine what size minimum platform is required to help reach a book's sales goals.

Get Your Numbers

Before you can do anything with platform, you need to uncover your qualitative numbers. Compile a spreadsheet of your social media followers across all platforms. List your YouTube and newsletter subscribers. Get the data on all your website and blog hits. Track down all your previous book sales and list out all your industry awards. If you're in radio, TV, or print, list those also.

Have you been published in large magazines, papers, or journals? Do you speak at schools, conferences, or churches? Do you have any credentials or degrees which qualify you to write your book? Mark those down also. You can use all of those to help you show platform.

What if My Platform Isn't High Enough Yet?

If your platform isn't big enough, don't fret. You CAN build platform. Authors are doing it right now as you read this. And you CAN build platform quickly; it doesn't have to take years or decades. But you have to work hard at it. An author who needs to build platform should be spending 60 percent of their time working on platform building, and 40 percent of their time writing and editing. It' doesn't matter how good your book is if you can't sell it. If you're a debut author and you're not building a platform, you're significantly decreasing your chances to get published. Always work on increasing your discoverability.

Do You Have to Have a Platform for Every Genre?

Yes and no. Nonfiction always requires platform, but the younger the audience is for the book, the less platform you will need to sell your book. An amazing, high concept book can still find a place in the fiction and children's market, but as with anything, a large platform is always helpful to convince a marketing and sales team to get behind your acquisitions editor and extend an offer to publish. If you want to work with the largest publishers, remember platform is king, and more often than not, it will play a significant role in determining whether or not your book gets offered a contract or how much advance (if any) you get offered.

Platform in the Children's Market

Children don't usually follow you on social media. For most genres in the juvenile market, you are trying to get the main book buyers to follow you—moms. Mothers buy the books for their children, and you want them to become your fans.

Platform and Advances

Platform also helps a publisher determine how many books they will likely sell upon release. Those metrics are plugged into a profitability matrix. That formula is used to determine how much advance and royalties an author can receive. Authors with large platforms have a higher potential for sales and thus will typically receive significantly more in advances. It pays to build your platform, literally.

Debut Platform

Debut authors can sometimes get a first-time pass to the platform game. They may be able to get a book deal without a lot of platform. But, the moment their book is published, it becomes platform—good or bad. If that book outperforms, it can help establish platform for the author and make it easier to sell future titles. If the book underperforms, it will hurt the author and make it much more difficult to sell future titles. If you can contract a book with smaller platform, make sure you sell it!

Platform is an ever-changing target. One thing is always true when it comes to platform—it never gets easier. Publishers continue to raise their platform targets for authors, and if you aren't working on platform, you will be falling behind those authors who do.

Lori Z. Scott

Lori Z. Scott writes children's fiction because she's like an atom. She makes everything up. She also has two quirky habits: chronic doodling and lame joke telling. Neither one impresses her boss, but they still somehow inspired Lori to write a best-selling book series and over 150 other publications.

What advice can you give to first-time authors in the Christian children's book realm?

Understand the calling and embrace it. If God has called you to write, write to the best of your ability.

I love what Erma Bombeck once said: When I stand before God at the end of my life, I would hope that I would not have a single bit of talent left, and could say, "I used everything you gave me." We don't have to be the best. We just have to do the best with what we have.

Do you have any nuggets of wisdom you can share about writing Christian children's books?

Consider writing short stories and poems for magazines. This is a great way to both hone your craft and earn publishing credits.

Are there any marketing tips you can share to encourage other children's book authors?

Speaking opportunities are a great way to market your book. • Create freebies and giveaways associated with your topic. Everyone loves a good deal. • Create activities and question guides that parents and teachers can use to go with your book. This added feature can be just that thing that draws in your audience. • Do blog and podcast tours. • Create a website. Use it to gather emails and a following, then send out a newsletter. • Reach out to organizations that might be interested in selling your product. For example, if your book is about creation, perhaps a zoo might carry it in their gift shop. • Create your own promotion team filled with people either willing to promote for you on their own social media sites or post reviews of your work.

Chapter 30

Query with Confidence
Michelle Medlock Adams

You only get one chance to make a good first impression, and a well-crafted query letter will accomplish just that. After writing hundreds of successful query letters over the course of my journalistic career, I've come up with the following "quick query tips" to help you query with confidence.

> - Be professional: Use Times New Roman, twelve-point type, and keep your text flush left. Just because you're querying a children's magazine or a children's book editor, don't get all goofy. For example, don't use glitter paper or scratch-and-sniff stickers to jazz up your query.
> - Always address your query letter to a specific person: You'll find that information in the various Writer's Market Guides, on publisher websites, and

- from faculty listings of various conferences. As a last resort, call the publisher or publication to find out an editor's name, spelling, and title, just to be sure.
- Indicate you've studied their publishing house or magazine: You might mention a book they've published or an article they have published or a section of their magazine that relates to your suggested text.
- Show how your proposed book/story fits with their publishing program/magazine.
- Go the extra mile: Always offer a little extra something in your query letter such as photographs to accompany your text or a parenting moment or "Fun Facts" or a fun sidebar to accompany your main magazine article. For a book query, you might offer various kinds of back matter. (See chapter 12 for more information about back matter.) The editors may not want all of those elements, but they will be impressed you offered them.
- Make sure the publisher/magazine you're querying is currently accepting submissions: Some only accept queries from unagented writers during certain months of the year. Also, some magazines work from theme lists so check to see if the magazine you're querying is working with such a list. If so, mention which month/theme your proposed story idea fits.
- Keep it concise: Try to keep your query to one page.
- Always include your credentials in your third paragraph: Even if you don't yet have any publishing credits, and even if you haven't yet won any writing awards, you still have something you can write in that third paragraph. Share why you're the perfect person to write that particular article or book. For

example, if you're pitching an article about Earning Money Over Summer Break, and you're a financial advisor or have a history in entrepreneurship, you can include that information in your letter. Or, if you have a really great source that you plan to quote in your article, mention that source.
- ➢ Make your last two lines work for you: The close to your query letter is just as important as your opening paragraph. Thank the editor for reading your query letter, and then offer to take on story ideas that their staff may not have time to generate. Tell the editor you are open to "Work for Hire" projects and that you'd like to be included in their "freelance pool of writers."

Once you've crafted an amazing query letter, make sure you keep good records, including the publication's name, the editor's name, the date you sent it, and when you expect to hear back from that publication. If the magazine/publisher accepts simultaneous submissions, pinpoint five or so publications that would be a good fit for your story idea/book and prepare letters for each one. I call this the "nail it and mail it" step. Just double-check that you've changed the editor's name and publication's address for each letter. And be sure you're sending that query the way the publication's guidelines instruct—via email or snail mail.

Lastly, try to keep ten query letters circulating at all times. I call this the "ten in rule," meaning I always have ten submissions out. Now, I may only have two different story ideas that I'm pitching, but I will pitch each one to five different magazines or publishing houses. Make sense?

OK, now go forth and query with confidence! Oh, and here's a sample query to get you started:

Christie R. Writer
1029 Victory Blvd.
Bloomington, IN 47401
(812) 332-0090
writer1@writer4Him.com www.writer4Him.com

August 12, 2020

Ms. Milly Krokey, Associate Editor
Beyond Blessed
1332 Circle Drive
Indianapolis, IN 46445

Dear Ms. Krokey:

With an upbeat country rock single, "I Miss You Like Crazy," on the radio and an Indiana University volleyball scholarship awaiting her this fall, eighteen-year-old Kerry Kuperton is one busy, multitalented girl. Given the nickname of "The Hoosier Hannah" (Montana) because of her fast-growing fan-base, she's a force to be reckoned with on and off the court. She has a big voice, a big talent, and a big heart for God. Kuperton grew up singing at church, and she continues to seek God's guidance as she navigates her way through the many opportunities flowing into her life.

I'd like to profile this talented teen for an upcoming issue of *Beyond Blessed*. I believe your readers will be interested in Kuperton's journey and challenged to step out and follow their own dreams. I plan on writing this piece much like a previous article that ran in your magazine: "Speed of Light!" that featured drag car racer Mallori Noninski. In addition, I have a sidebar/pullout box that lists five pieces of advice that have impacted Kuperton's life. And, I have several pictures I took of Kuperton when she recently performed at a charity event in Bloomington. I'm happy to send those via email—just say the word.

Let me tell you a little about my writing background. I am an award-winning journalist, earning first-place honors from the Associated Press, the Hoosier State Press Association, and the Society of Professional Journalists. I have written more than fifteen hundred articles for newspapers and magazines across the country, including: *American Cheerleader, American Cheerleader Jr., Brio, Sweet 16!* and *Writer's Digest.* In addition, I am the author of over one hundred books with close to four million copies sold. Please know that I also work on assignment, so if you need a writer to tackle a story, I hope you'll consider contacting me. I look forward to hearing from you. Thank you for your time.

Sincerely,
Christie R. Writer

Make Your Cover Letter Count!
Cyle Young

A proper cover letter is essential in connecting with a prospective agent or editor. I have rejected countless submissions because of an unclear, immature, or unprofessional letter of introduction from the author. A cover letter is your first introduction to an industry professional; you don't want to make a bad impression—you may not get a second chance.

Publishing is a business, so treat it as such. Introduce yourself to the editor or agent you are emailing, and be sure to give them all the pertinent information about the work you are pitching or proposing. If it's a book, make sure to state the proposed title, word count, target age group, and genre.

Once you've given the basic information, give the editor a taste of your "voice." Share a blurb about your work that is well-written and crafted to engage the reader. You want the agent or editor to open your attached files and keep reading. Don't skimp on your blurb; if you do, you will regret it later.

End your letter with information about yourself, but not too much. You can share a longer bio in your proposal, but it helps to know who is writing the work. If you have a large platform or following, make sure to highlight that as fast as possible. Publishing is currently a platform business, and platform never hurts.

Make sure you sign the letter and be careful not to be too wordy or cute. Have another professional read your letter before you send it out and get their feedback.

Take a look at this sample.

Sample Cover Letter

XXXXX,

I have attached XXXXX by popular food blogger and influencer, XXXXX.

[Insert Book Description]

A breakdown of XXXXX platform and food industry connections is contained in the proposal. Some of the highlights of her online platform include 750,000 monthly pageviews, 609,000 Facebook followers, 55,000 Instagram followers. She also has 7.2 million monthly viewers on Pinterest. XXXXX is friends with many well-known cookbook authors and food influencers who have already confirmed to endorse and help market this book, XXXXXX (XXXXXX 2.9 million IG followers) and XXXXXX (XXXXXX 1.2 million IG followers), among others.

For over a decade, XXXXX, the full-time blogger and recipe developer at XXXXXX, has inspired readers to step up their hosting and hospitality. XXXXX has garnered hundreds of thousands of fans at www.authorswebsite.com. She enjoys hiking, camping in her family's Sprinter van, traveling, hosting parties, sharing hospitality wherever she goes, and bringing people together. XXXXX lives in XXXXXX, with her family and two dogs.

Thank you for reviewing this simultaneous submission!

Sincerely,
Cyle Young

Chapter 31

Proposals
Cyle Young

A well-written proposal sells your book. Editors and agents review proposals to find all the information they need to determine whether or not a book is a viable project worth an investment of time, energy, or capital. You want to spend a considerable amount of time crafting a proposal that clearly communicates your project, your passion, your expertise, and your market.

The proposal process begins with individually shaping the required pieces. When each part of a proposal has been written and edited, it is time to pull them together into a sales document that helps you catch the interest of acquisition agents and editors.

Pieces of a Proposal *(in no particular order)*

Cover page
This page gives the project title, word count, and genre. It should also have all of your contact information—so the agent or editor can contact you if they are interested.

Header or Footer
In the header or footer, put your last name, one form of contact, and the work title. This is in case the editor or agent prints out the document and the pages get separated. It allows them to get ahold of you, even if they lose your contact page.

Table of Contents
This isn't required, but if your proposal is erring on the long side, you may want to include it to help agents and editors navigate it more quickly.

Blurb
A good blurb catches someone's attention and makes them want to read more. Many blurbs are used from promotional material by the marketing team, as back cover copy, or for a book jacket. Take time to make your blurb sing.

Overview
An overview reveals the bird's eye picture of your book. It allows an agent or editor to gain a high level of perspective on what your book is about and what the need is for the target audience. A good overview can help sell your book, and you should spend time researching this section.

Proposed Format
Books come in various shapes, formats, and sizes. The proposed format section allows you to communicate your intended thoughts about what the project is going to look like. You can communicate your thoughts about trim size, length, illustration, format, etc.

Biography
When agents and editors care about you, they are naturally more inclined to care about your writing. In less than a page, share about your life, your credentials, your family, and any other information that helps them determine why you are the right person to write this book.

Speaking Engagements
Speakers sell books. If you are consistently speaking in front of audiences or groups of people, make sure to share a list of booked engagements and anticipated audience sizes. If you know your audience sell-through numbers—the average percentage of your audience that purchases your books—share that information also.

Previous Publication & Sales History
Your previous book sales are a good barometer of your reader base. Include all your previously published titles, self-published, hybrid published, or traditionally published. Detail your sales figures for each title, and if you have lower sales, provide a realistic explanation of why the sales are low and what you have done to change your platform since releasing those works.

Platform
This section is full of empirical numbers. Numbers of followers on social media, size of your mailing list, website

hits, etc. This section helps a publisher understand your reach and discoverability in a crowded marketplace. Publishers want to sell books, and a large or growing platform can help them gather those sales.

Endorsements

Endorsements are helpful—if the editor or agent knows who the person endorsing your book is. Your local writing partner is not an adequate endorsement. Include endorsements from large platform individuals or organizations (that you actually know and have connection with). Potential endorsements from strangers are worthless in a proposal. Seek out endorsers who can help you sell books and if you get some, include them in your proposal.

Comparative Works

Authors shirk this section all the time, but it is one of the most helpful sections to assist the agent or editor with understanding the market for your book. It also reveals whether or not you know your potential market. Compare and contrast your book to eight to ten comparative works that are competition for your book. At least five of those comparatives should have been published within the last five years.

Target Audience

Who's going to buy your book? Hint, it's not every person who ever lives, and it's not every woman over eighteen years old. Be specific. Hone in and describe the segment of readers who are most likely going to be interested in your book. Makes sure the audience is not too niche that it's not substantial enough to purchase enough books for a publisher to make a profit. And make sure it's not too large that you don't have a clear target audience.

Marketing & Publicity
Describe your plan for assisting the publisher with getting your book in front of target buyers. The days of the publisher doing all the sales and marketing are long gone. Every author has to help a publisher sell a title. Your marketing and publicity plan will be used to help a publisher determine the viability of investing in your project and can potentially get the publishing houses marketing, publicity, and sales teams excited about working on your future book.

This section should be full of things you ARE going to do and ARE doing. Describe how you are going to market and publicize your book before, during, and after release.

Synopsis or Chapter by Chapter Summary
A synopsis is for fiction proposals. In less than three pages, share the plot of your book. Include the growth plan for your protagonist and share any side plots or character arcs that are essential for understanding the book. Don't leave a cliffhanger at the end—that can lead to rejection. Editors and agents want to know where the book is going, and they want to know how you tie it up in the end. Don't rush a synopsis; this could be the first real taste of your writing, so make sure the synopsis is clear and still has your voice.

You include a fleshed out Chapter by Chapter Summary in nonfiction proposals. A chapter by chapter summary gives an editor or agent a complete overview of your book. It details all the major points and themes of each chapter and reveals how they help to fulfill the central promise of the book. Be thorough. You don't have to be clever or cute in this section, just get the details clear and don't leave anything out.

Sample Chapters

For a board or picture book, you include the entire manuscript.

For a fiction proposal, include the first three chapters—no prologue.

For a nonfiction proposal, include the first three chapters—no introduction

> **Jennifer Froelich**
>
> *Do you have any nuggets of wisdom you can share about writing Christian children's books?*
>
> Develop a thick skin, be your own worst critic, and your own biggest champion. Never sell out on your faith in order to sell out of books. Be genuine to your voice and ask God for wisdom in all that you write.
>
> *Are there any platform-building tips you can share to encourage other children's book authors?*
>
> On social media, it is important to engage genuinely with others. Have conversations, make sure you are giving as much as you are asking for. Do not get caught up in numbers or share-for-sharing or review-for-reviewing schemes. Your platform will build over time, but there are rarely any substantive quick builds.
>
> *What has been your greatest joy in your CRA Children's publishing journey?*
>
> I am genuinely overjoyed when I chat with readers who have loved my stories. When they begin to tell me how much they adore my characters, they

Proposals

often start to describe traits that I wasn't sure were coming across on the page the way they were in my head. Bringing those characters to life for others to enjoy is the greatest joy of all.

Chapter 32

Writing and Selling to Christian Magazines
Lori Z. Scott

Every day in my elementary classroom, I teach a roomful of hopeful writers. These pint-sized scholars share a dream to publish their own books one day. Yet not once have I heard them utter, "I want to write for a magazine."

Like my students, many writers focus their efforts on book publication. But we shouldn't overlook the value of writing for magazines. In my career, the time I invested composing for this media provided me with real-world experiences on the business side of writing while helping me hone my craft. In addition, it gave me a notebook full of publishing credits. When I "graduated" from this classroom, I carried every lesson I learned with me all the way to a best-selling, ten-book children's series.

Lesson 1: Does Your Submission Fit Their Mission?

Sometimes I assign writing prompts to my students. But no matter how sweet the tale they turn in, if it's not on topic, it affects their grade.

Magazine editors deal with this too. Writers often submit well-written articles that are ill-fitted for the publication. Lynn Gilliam, editor for *Pockets* magazine pinpoints the problem. "The biggest single submission mistake many writers make is just not knowing enough about the publication to which they're submitting their work. If you're experiencing consistent rejection, try taking a closer look at the publications you're targeting to make sure you really have a good understanding of what they're looking for."

Use submission guidelines like a teacher uses a grading rubric. By checking each box to make sure you've fulfilled every requirement, you increase the likelihood of getting published. This tactic works for magazines AND book publishers.

Lesson 2: Theme

Love. Hope. Peace. The most powerful children's books focus on a single takeaway value or theme. Writing for magazines teaches you how to weave that element into your story. Many publications devote an entire issue to one central idea. They often post theme lists online, sometimes with suggestions on the type of approach they desire. The work they select must support that topic. That means when an editor picks between two equally eloquent pieces, the one that best fits the theme will win every time.

Lesson 3: Deadlines, Word Counts, and Queries! Oh My!

Unlike books, which can take years to go from idea to market, magazine publishers move fast. Monthly deadlines force writers to set goals and discipline themselves. In effect, it mimics a five-minute fact quiz. If you don't finish it on time, you miss the grade. How does that help book writers? By training yourself to meet a magazine's tight deadline, you're better equipped to make last-minute changes to your manuscript.

Besides working against a clock, writers must adhere to a publication's specific word count requirements. Like math problems, students work until they determine the correct number; writers must select stronger verbs and trim unnecessary phrases to fit the desired word count. However, rather than weaken the final product, this exercise often strengthens it. Authors must master writing succinct compositions that demand the audience's attention ... a skill essential to book writing too.

Unless otherwise stated, include an appropriate cover letter with your fiction submission. If it's a non-fiction article, a simple query letter will do. Even if editors don't like your idea, they may be enticed by your writing and offer you a different assignment. (If they do, say YES!)

Focus on the Family editor Marianne Hering confirms this approach. "For me, the query letter for the article was merely an introduction to their writing. If the topic was anywhere close to something I'd use and the query (now a pitch) was well-crafted, I asked for the article. Even if I didn't want that particular article in a dire way, I wanted to see if the person could write."

Lesson 4: Discoverability

Authors shouldn't just consider magazine writing as a classroom. When it comes to exposure, our glossy friends have a distinct advantage. While the first print for a book typically runs five thousand copies, a magazine can reach tens or hundreds of thousands more people with a single issue. Plus, consider where readers find magazines. They lurk in libraries, bookstores, waiting rooms at doctor offices, hair salons, fitness centers, airports, websites, coffee lounges, car repair shops, or even the foyers of apartment complexes.

Besides gaining publicity, seasoned authors use magazine articles to establish themselves as an expert on their topic. This can lead to more writing (or even speaking) opportunities and more income. Book editors also like to see those credits in your resume. It demonstrates you can write something people want to read.

Lesson 5: Tip and Tricks

I've published over one hundred fifty poems, short stories, devotions, essays, and puzzles for children and teen magazines. I believe my success stems from following a few practices.

- ➢ Read the submission guidelines. And then follow them exactly.
- ➢ Familiarize yourself with your publication's style, content, and mission. You can often find back issues online. Otherwise, request a copy.
- ➢ Be flexible. If an editor asks you to revise and resubmit your article, take any feedback they provide to heart. Don't be afraid to cut favorite sections to suit their needs.
- ➢ Read your submission out loud. When I read to my

students, their reactions reveal a lot. What they found interesting or boring. What jokes worked well or fell flat. What information needs clarification. At the very least, read it out loud to yourself.
- ➤ Submit fillers. Many editors claim this is the best trick to break into your target market. Magazines typically need more fillers than stories, raising your chances of being selected.
- ➤ Fillers include puzzles, poems, or sometimes short prayers.

Class Dismissed

In summary, don't overlook the value of writing for magazines. Instead, offer this media the respect it deserves. If you're like me, each byline you earn will shine in your heart like a gold star on a test. It can also help prepare you for the next level in your career, including your dream book.

Amanda Flinn

Amanda Flinn is an award-winning author, blogger and book nerd. She lives in Southeast Missouri with her husband, three boys, their new rescue pup, and a furry chinchilla. Her debut children's books, *Yoga Baby* and *The Maker* release in 2020. To learn more about her family and recent writing projects, visit www.amandaflinn.com.

What advice can you give to first-time CRA authors?

Think outside the box. So many of us want to write a book, but there are other routes to publishing that need to be explored along the way. Look into magazine articles, journals, the local newspaper, blogging—anything that gets you writing and fuels your fire. The process of idea to manuscript to physical book can take years. It's nice to have multiple projects going at the same time to help fill the wait. Plus, your first idea might not be your best one, and everything improves with practice. Having a well-rounded portfolio demonstrates that you are serious about writing, no matter what final form your story takes.

Do you have any nuggets of wisdom you can share about writing Christian children's book authors?

Most people will tell you to read a lot of children's books and get to know the market. I completely agree with those tips, but ultimately, you need to write the story that is on your heart, the one that only you can tell. Don't force a book just because it fits with today's trends. Write something that makes you come alive. Write something that you love. Write something you will be proud of in twenty years.

Are there any marketing tips you can share to encourage other children's book authors?

Start marketing yourself as an established writer, long before you ever have a book contract. Get to know your audience and be a resource for them. Write blog posts, talk about your journey, and put yourself out there. Succeed in front of people and fail in front of people. Books will come and go, but if your audience believes in you as an authentic person, one that is kind and helpful and good, then not only have you increased your chance of book sales, but you have made a slew of lifelong friends.

Chapter 33

Author Visits
Shannon Anderson

What could be more exciting than getting your book published? How about the chance to share it with the very audience you created it for? There are many reasons I love doing author visits. Dan Gutman once said that a good school visit can earn you two hundred to five hundred fans all in one afternoon! You can also build your author platform with key readers and purchasers in the children's book industry (teachers and librarians). Of course, you may have the chance to sell your books at the visit, and hopefully, you inspire a future little author or illustrator.

The success of your visit is dependent on a lot of factors. As an author, I've had the opportunity to visit over one hundred schools. I'm a third-grade teacher and have some insight from the school perspective to offer as well. Here are a few of the questions I get asked most often:

Q: How do you get invited to schools?

A: When my first book was published, I started out by doing presentations at schools in my own town. Then, I researched schools within a one-hour radius that would consider me a "local author" of sorts. You can email the principal and/or media specialist of these schools. These are key people who would offer these types of programs to students. (Almost all school websites offer staff directories with email addresses listed.)

You can also contact your high school and college friends with kids. You're more likely to catch the attention of a principal if you're able to say that you know the family of a student who attends there.

Although I started out locally and networked through people I knew, most of my "gigs" now are a direct result of my presentations for teachers at conferences. I often present, "Be an Amazing Writing Teacher" and share that I love to motivate students to write through my author visits too. When I return from a conference, I usually have emails from schools requesting more information.

Other ways to get invitations are by sharing your author visits on social media, maintaining an author website and blog, creating and sending out brochures about your visits, joining a speakers' list, and joining organizations that support children's literature. For example, being a part of a local or state reading association, or joining the Society of Children's Book Writers and Illustrators. These organizations allow you to network with other teachers and authors regularly.

Q: What do you do during your presentation?

A: The goal of my presentation is to be a writing cheerleader. I want to motivate students to see writing as fun and to help them become better writers. I start out by sharing *my* excitement for writing. I show pictures of me writing in my writing cottage, learning at writing camps and workshops, teaching writing, and working on books. (I include pictures of my pets, kids, home, and favorite writing spots.)

I share what motivated me to write each of my books. The kids love to hear the backstory and personal connections to each book. This allows me to also talk about "Author's Purpose," which is a reading standard in the elementary grade levels.

I make a big deal out of my four big "secret" writing tips. This hooks the kids because they want to know this "confidential" information. My tips are:

1. Read
2. Write
3. Learn from others
4. Never give up

After I expand on each tip, with personal experience, I show them a peek at what it's like to be an author. I show author visits, book deliveries, book signings, reading to kids, and all of the fun parts of the job. Then, I remind them that it's also a lot of work to get something published. I show pictures of brainstorming, working on page turns, editing, and approving sketches.

I wrap up with a chance for kids to volunteer and share what they remember about the four writing tips. I have a prop for each of these for students to hold. (It makes a great picture opt for the teachers.) If there is any time remaining, I take a few questions.

Your presentation will probably be different than mine because your goals and your books will be different. Be sure students know you are excited to be there and that you love what you do. Once they know you care, they will care about what you know.

Q: What should I charge for an author visit?

A: This answer depends on many things. First off, as a published author and presenter, you are a professional and should be paid. Schools will value your visit more if they are investing in the presentation. You are also taking away time from your writing or other business to contribute your services to a school.

That being said, there are circumstances when you may not charge for a visit. For example, when you are first starting out, when you change your presentation and need a practice run, or are presenting for a cause or charity. You may even negotiate a deal with a school that if they buy X number of books, they receive a free author visit in return.

If you *are* charging for your visit, the amount can vary from author to author. Some authors charge as little $100, and some make over $2,000 on a whole day visit. There is no set rate, but those earning more typically have multiple books in traditional publication, have won awards, have great reviews, and/or are well-known in their field. The amount can also vary based on how many presentations the school would like you to do in one day. Don't forget to ask for reimbursement for travel and lodging if applicable too.

Q: Once a school has invited me, what do I do next?

A: There are many details you will want to iron out prior to your visit:

- ➢ Exactly what fee will be charged for the presentation and travel?
- ➢ What are the travel arrangements, if applicable?

- If driving, where should you park, and what door should you enter through?
- What is the schedule for the day of your visit, including lunch?
- Can you sell your books at the visit? Can you send a book order form prior to your visit for students? Will the school take care of book sales?
- What grade levels and how many students will be there?
- What technology equipment do you need? (Projector, microphone, etc.)

As you can see, successful visits can be rewarding, but also take time to set up and execute well. With practice and time, you'll be an expert at sharing your writing and excitement for the books you have created for your audience.

Chapter 34

Networking
Cyle Young

The publishing world is not as big as you may think it is. It's actually a rather small world where most of the major players, professionals, and authors all know each other, at least at an acquaintance level.

It pays to invest in building relationships with other authors, agents, and editors. Many Christian writing conferences and retreats allow you to sign up for one-on-one appointments with their faculty. Agents and editors often comprise the faculty at these conferences, and over time you can network with some of the industry's biggest decision-makers. Try to get to a writer's conference so you can build relationships.

You never know which conversation will be the divine appointment that leads a future publishing contract or lifelong friendship. Take time to invest in connecting with other writers and industry veterans. Not only are these wonderful people a wealth of resources and information, they may be your best source of encouragement when you inevitably face rejection and discouragement. Even the best authors get rejected from time to time.

Publishing is an industry where even shy people can connect through the common medium of the written word. If you can't make it to conferences or writing retreats, try interacting with other authors, agents, and editors on social media. Just make sure that you aren't pushy. And remember, it's easiest to connect with people and build relationships with others when you are genuinely interested in them, and you aren't always trying to pitch or sell your book. Taking an honest interest and caring about others will get you much further in Christian publishing than just trying to sell your manuscript.

Chapter 35

Six Tips to Make Your Book Signing Successful
Michelle Medlock Adams

You're at your book signing, Sharpie in hand, ready to sign one of the dozens of copies displayed on your table, and no one shows up. Even though you're positioned in front of Starbucks, people find a path around you to avoid having to make eye contact with you in their quest for java. Ever been there? It can be the longest afternoon of your life; trust me, I speak from experience.

But it doesn't have to be if you follow these six strategies for a successful book signing.

1. **Make it an event!** Though authors get pretty excited about book signings, most people do not. So, make it an exciting event—not just a signing. For example, when I was planning a book signing event for my book, *Get Your Spirit On! Devotions for*

Cheerleaders I went all out. I ordered "Swag bag" items that cheerleaders ages eight to twelve would love such as: cheer bows, slap bracelets, a notebook and pencil with the name of my book on them, and a cheerleading tote bag that matched my book's cover and had "Get Your Spirit On!" printed on it. I advertised on all social media outlets that the first twenty-five people to purchase a book would receive the adorable swag bag, and that's not all. Knowing that high school cheerleaders are royalty to younger cheerleaders, I asked two local Varsity cheerleaders to come in uniform and help hand out swag bags and be available for photos. I added in a few cake pops tied up with spirit ribbons, and my boring book signing became a festive event! I also contacted all of the elementary and middle school cheer coaches in the area and let them know about the event. As a result, I had a great turnout and sold many books. And, we all did a few cheers. It was a perfect day.

2. **Get the word out ahead of time!** Make an attractive meme on Canva or Word Swag or whatever creative app you like best, promoting your upcoming book signing several weeks ahead of the event. (You might even do a countdown!) Post on all of your social media sites. But don't stop there! Use what we call "Borrowed Platform" and ask some of your friends with larger followings to share your meme. Make sure your meme has all of the pertinent information about your event—time, date, location, etc. You'll also want to be sure you use a "sizer" when creating your memes so that your cute creations will fit perfectly on Facebook, Twitter, Pinterest, Instagram, and LinkedIn. Unfortunately, it's not a "one size fits all" social media world. Each

platform has its own sizing preferences.
3. **Write a press release and send it out!** Once you've written a press release about your upcoming event, contact the Community Relations Coordinator (CRC) at the bookstore where you're having the event, and see if he/she has a media list (contact names and numbers of local media) that you could use when sending out your release.

   If the CRC doesn't have a media list compiled, make sure you ask which TV and radio stations you should contact, as well as which area newspapers and magazines might be interested. Working closely with the store's CRC is always a good idea. I've found if I let the CRC know I'm doing all I can to promote the event, that CRC will become excited and promote the event with even more fervor.
4. **Be friendly and proactive!** Too many authors simply sit at their book table and smile as potential book buyers pass by, but that's not the best way to run your event. Ask the CRC if you could read your book back in the children's area several times throughout your allotted time. If that request gets approved, then ask the CRC to announce your upcoming readings in the children's area a few minutes before each one, adding that the author is on hand to personalize and sign copies. Parents love that!
5. **Lure book buyers to your table!** So, how do you lure potential book buyers to your table? Have an attractive setup—a pretty tablecloth that matches your book, easels to display your books, free bookmarks (Vistaprint is a very affordable way to make bookmarks of your book's cover), candy or cookies, your business cards or fliers, a freebie of some sort like a coloring sheet to complement

your book, etc.

With my book, *C Is for Christmas* (Little Lamb Books), my publisher created bookmarks and stickers to hand out to the children—both were a huge hit! As children walked past my table, I'd offer them a free bookmark and sticker. Who doesn't love a freebie? That almost always lured the children and their parents over to my table, and usually, it resulted in a book sale. I also offered candy canes, which went right along with my book. You might also want to add a signup sheet on your table, asking for the parents' emails in case they'd like to be notified of your future books and events. (That's a great way to build your email list.)

6. **Have a Giveaway!** I always put together a gift basket with fun stuff that relates to the book I'm signing. (You don't want to give away a copy of the book because you want people to buy your book.) For example, when I signed *Dinosaur Devotions* at an area bookstore, I created the cutest gift basket filled with Dinosaur egg candy, dinosaur socks, a dinosaur pencil, dinosaur fun fact cards, a stuffed dino, and a dinosaur picture frame. I tied it all up in ivory tulle and a gorgeous green bow. It was eye-catching on my book table, and it caused people to stop by my table to enter the drawing. Again, once I was able to get them to my book table, I almost always made a sale.

Remember, your enthusiasm about your book is contagious! Be excited, and you'll create an atmosphere of excitement, and that's attractive to potential book buyers.

Art Ginolfi
Author of *The Tiny Star* and *The Tiny Snowflake*—originally published by Tommy Nelson and re-released by Skyhorse.

What advice can you give to first-time authors?
Be original and authentic.

Do you have any nuggets of wisdom you can share about writing Christian children's books?
Know what publishers are looking to publish.

Are there any marketing tips you can share to encourage other children's book authors?
Once you get the book published, be prepared to market it, and generate publicity.

Chapter 36

Winning Strategies to Get Your Books in the Hands of Young Readers
Mary Morgan

One of the best ways to reach your targeted audience is to go where they go—craft shows and conferences. Spending one or two days of a weekend under a canopy or in a convention hall takes dedication and determination to make the best use of your time and the money you invested in the registration fee. Over the past eight years and twenty thousand books later, I have learned what it takes for me to make a sale.

Be confident your product is the best you can make it AND that your customers need it! When you are convinced of that, you sell with enthusiasm. I have eight titles in my National Park Mystery series for pre-teens.

I know the content is educational, and families can take my books to the parks and use them as a travel guide for adventures. Colorful covers invite kids to pick up the book and are drawn into the suspense when they read the summary on the back. The plots are age-appropriate, and fourteen-point type size is pleasing to elementary children. Parents are willing to buy a book their child gets excited about. And for younger brothers and sisters, preschoolers giggle their way through *The Runaway Lawnmower* while finding the hidden worm and following Lucky's adventures around the neighborhood. The Spanish version won a national Moonbeam Children's Book Award, adding a winner to the collection.

To be convincing as a salesperson, you have to sell yourself. Work hard to make your appearance the best you can be. I write for children, so I dress in 'happy colors' – pink, red, yellow, purple, blue – many of which are their favorite colors. I smile, act perky, and show an interest in everyone who walks by. I don't sit in a chair scrolling on my phone but stand right behind the table ready to engage someone in conversation. "Is your child a reader?" Or to a child, I might ask, "Do you like mysteries?" I'm always ready with a quick 'yes' when someone asks if I have visited the parks I write about. And with a twinkle in my eye, I tell them their family needs one of my books.

Make a good impression with a great looking display. Color is key. Books based in national parks call for red, white, and blue table coverings and glittery garland. The books stand up, facing out to the crowd, at eye-level of my intended readers. Behind our display is an eight-foot retractable sign of me sitting on a boulder at the edge of the Grand Canyon. It is bigger-than-life, and it opens the door to natural conversations about the series and how families can benefit from a trip to the parks.

Children don't control the purse-strings, so you need to rely on eye-appeal. To help sell *The Runaway Lawnmower*, I have a toy lawnmower and stuffed green worms (available to buy) sitting next to the book display. Little ones see the lawnmower, want to play with it, and then I show them the book with a hidden worm on each page. With a worm in one hand and a book in the other, preschoolers take home a delightful set.

Given today's concern of talking to strangers, I developed a strategy of talking safely to children. I print bookmarks of each book on cardstock with the book cover and description on one side and my contact information on the other. As families walk by, I offer the bookmark to the child while making eye contact and talking to the parent. When parents realize you have something safe for their child, they let them pick up a book and flip through it. Pictures of real children, who I use as the characters, are in the back. It's another winning strategy for making a personal connection with a reader.

In addition to bookmarks, information sheets about the books are available in an acrylic magazine holder. Families find them to be helpful when choosing a book. Some are interested in history, while others like books set in a particular location, and travelers look for books with a vacation destination in mind. Having your contact information or how to order more books is invaluable once they are home. And for another venue, teachers and PTO parents are on the lookout for authors to visit their schools. These sheets have helped get me speaking engagements as a Michigan author opening up another market of readers.

To my delight, one of my best markets is Home School Conferences. Most homeschool children are voracious readers, and their parents try to screen what they read. My books are geared toward the general (secular) market, so there is no mention of God, but the Golden Rule and Christian ethics are woven through the storyline. At homeschool conferences, I post a sign which reads Christian Worldview, Safe-Reading for Children, and mention that the real characters are homeschool children from Lansing. Parents feel my connection with them and buy books by the sets. An added bonus is, many homeschool families travel to national parks as part of their curriculum, so use my books as a guide and then send me postcards.

End the sale on a high note. I offer to personalize and autograph each book and then ask if the child would like their picture taken by my big sign. Rarely do I ever get turned down since kids love meeting an author. Most parents have smartphones and are pleased to have this extra bonus for their child.

Making a book sale is always a thrill. Knowing something you created has the potential to influence someone to read, learn, travel, and possibly try something new, has its own reward. If you have the passion, you can do it. As convincingly as I can say it, if it happened to me, it can happen to you.

Chapter 37

Self-Publishing Your Books
Catherine Jones Payne

More than a million books are self-published each year.[1] Most of these self-published books don't become breakout best sellers. Based on my experience in the industry as an editor and a self-published writer, I can tell you that most self-published books hamstring themselves with unsaleable concepts, poorly done covers, or inadequate editing.

If you're thinking of self-publishing in the Christian market, how can *you* set your book up for success? There are never any guarantees in this industry, but carefully considering the market and professionally producing a

---

[1] "Self-Publishing Grew 40 Percent in 2018, New Report Reveals." Bowker. October 15, 2019. http://www.bowker.com/news/2019/Self-Publishing-Grew-40-Percent-in-2018-New-Report--Reveals.html

book will go a long way toward helping you stand out from the crowd.

And, of course, as Christians, we're not just about making money or selling copies. Art reveals truth. Our books have a mission, whether we include overt faith content or not. And so we must be committed to the pursuit of excellence in all our endeavors, including in how we publish our books—"as if working for the Lord, not for human masters" (Colossians 3:23 NIV).

So You've Written a Book . . . Now What?

First, develop your publishing plan. Consider whether this is a project you want to self-publish. This is, first and foremost, a business decision. Do a lot of market research. Find out what it takes to do well as a self-published author *in your genre*—does the genre have self-published success stories, or is it dominated by traditional publishers? The industry can change fast, but as I write this, self-published YA stands a much better chance than self-published MG. Find out what's happening *right now*, and use that information to guide you.

There's no right or wrong answer to the question of how to publish—but you don't want to make a choice based on one of the common **myths** about self-publishing.

Myth #1: I should self-publish because I haven't been able to get representation.

If you've gotten a steady stream of rejections from agents, self-publishing *may* still be right for you. But look at the *content* of those rejections. If you're hearing repeatedly, "I love the story and your writing, but I just can't sell it right now," your story might be a great candidate for self-publishing. But there are no shortcuts in this industry. If agents are saying, "You need to work on your craft," don't jump ship to self-publishing. Spend some more time learning, practicing, and improving, so that you can release a great debut—however it's published.

Myth #2: I should self-publish because my project is too niche for a publisher.

If your goal is just to publish a book, that's fine! But if your goal is to *sell* copies—if you want to do this professionally—you'll need to write a book that resonates with readers. There are trends and tropes that sell self-published books to readers, just as there are trends and tropes that land contracts. Lots of good potential projects won't get a contract—but most projects need to be refined before they'll resonate with a broad audience.

Self-Publishing Professionally

Once you've decided to self-publish, the fun part begins! You, as an author-publisher, get to release your book into the world. This is exciting! But proceed with caution.

I sell a lot of books at in-person events. Most of the books I see in the vendor hall don't look professionally produced. You can tell the author DIYed the cover or cobbled together oddly spaced formatting in Microsoft Word.

Be prepared to invest in your book. You made a business decision to self-publish. Businesses require some capital to get started. Resist the temptation to hire someone because they gave you the cheapest quote. If you want to sell books, you need to grab readers. You're not just a writer—you're a publisher, and you have to think like one. That means hiring professionals to help produce the book.

At minimum, you'll want pros for **cover design** and **copy editing**. To take your book to the next level, you'll also want people for **developmental editing, line editing,**

print formatting, and **ebook formatting**.

Let's talk about each of these in brief:

Your **cover** is the most important part of your book. You can have an engaging story with a great blurb and phenomenal editing, but if your cover looks unprofessional or is not a good fit for your genre, you won't reach readers. A cover artist needs to be capable of professional art and typography that *hits your genre tropes* and attracts your ideal reader. Unless you're a graphic design professional—and maybe not even then—do not design this yourself!

I always recommend hiring at least one **editor** to look over the manuscript. I have a team of three to four editors for mine because it's important to me that I release books as professional as anything coming out of a Big 5 house (Simon and Schuster, Penguin Random House, Hachette, HarperCollins, Macmillan). If you must choose an editor for only one stage, pick copy editing—but make sure you work with *lots* of beta readers (who are not your mom) and learn *everything* you can about story structure.

Formatting is something I choose to hire out, but it *can* be a place where you cut corners to save money. There are programs specific to book formatting you can use. Make sure you do your research on what is normal and expected for formatting in your genre!

Sell Books

Once you've produced and published a professional book, congratulations! That's a huge milestone! But there's still the hard work of selling it. There are innumerable resources out there on marketing self-published books—you'll want to put together a cohesive marketing plan and stick to it.

But here, I want to encourage you to seek out a market specific to Christian children's books, because you won't hear this everywhere else—sell at homeschool conventions. As a homeschool graduate myself, these conventions are some of my favorite in-person events. Homeschoolers are often voracious readers, and parents are always looking for Christian-made, age-appropriate books for their kids. At homeschool conventions, I've had the privilege of praying with overwhelmed moms and watching tweens' and teens' faces light up at the sight of YA fantasy their parents approve of. Moms will even hug me because they're excited about the books!

Work toward excellence, because you're working for God. Pray often. Do all your research. Produce a professional book. There's no guarantee of a best seller—the industry just doesn't work like that—but you'll have put yourself head and shoulders above most of the crowd. And of course, at the end of the day, it's not just about selling copies. More rewarding even than moving books is the knowledge that we've done our best with the mission God has placed on our hearts—an inspiration to keep learning, growing, and improving, to pursue excellence in all we do.

Chapter 38

The Differences Between the Markets: Christian to General
Cyle Young

Not all markets are the same. And you shouldn't treat them the same either. The Christian market (better known as the Christian Retail Association or CRA, formerly known as the Christian Booksellers Association or CBA) is drastically different than the general market (American Booksellers Association or ABA). In 2017, the StatShot survey from the American Association of Publishers estimated the CRA makes up around 15-20 percent of all trade titles sold each year in the US. That's about the same impact as the entire United Kingdom market. The survey also revealed that books with religious and inspirational themes were some of the overall best sellers in the entire industry. But even though a few religious titles climbed into the top ranks of the market, the CRA and ABA markets have different publishing focuses, unique reader demands, and sometimes opposite ideals.

Carving out success in either market requires a savvy author to study the trends, write with excellence, and craft books that publishers can't resist putting in print. These challenges can be made easier by deciphering the difference between the ABA and CRA markets and writing specifically to each market.

Money Versus Mission

The number one driving force in the ABA is money. Profits determine potential in the general market. If a publisher doesn't believe that a book can reach a certain sales threshold, the book will not be offered a contract. It's a cut and dry process. General market publishers exist to make money for their owners, shareholders, and investors. There are always some outliers and exceptions to this viewpoint, but when speaking of the largest companies—the Big 5 (Simon and Schuster, Penguin Random House, Hachette, Harper Collins, Macmillan)—this perspective holds true.

Christian publishers aren't driven by the almighty dollar. They exist to share their Christian worldview and beliefs with society and to provide resources to Christian readers. Even though Christian publishers still need to make money to exist, money is not their sole or main focus. Publishers in the CRA can also vary significantly in their Christian belief system, so not every CRA company shares the same viewpoint or perspective on Christianity. But even though they may differ to certain degrees theologically, CRA publishers function in very similar ways with their message or mission taking priority over money.

Reader Bases

General market companies have the advantage that their reader bases consist of ALL readers, even Christians who read CRA books. But the reverse isn't true in the CRA. Non-Christian readers will not purchase and read CRA books. An exclusivity of belief systems limits the readership of the CRA and ultimately caps the potential in the Christian market based upon the amount of Christians who purchase CRA books.

ABA books like *Harry Potter*, *Twilight*, and *In Search of Truth* have been able to attract Christian readers as well as non-Christian readers. No cap exists on the general market and every title launches into the market with unlimited potential. Publishers hope that each book will sell millions of copies and become the next *Harry Potter*. Because of a significantly smaller reader base in the CRA, most books will never sell enough copies to reach the all-important lists like NY Times Bestseller, USA Today Bestseller, or WSJ Bestseller.

High Concept Versus Traditional

One of the biggest differences between the ABA and CRA is the juxtaposition between high concept ideas and traditional content. The general market strategy is often to push the envelope with new ideas or high concepts. High concept moves beyond a unique idea and instead paints a bold picture in the reader's mind of what the book is about even before he or she has cracked the first page. Young adult books like *13 Reasons Why* and *I'd Tell You I Love You, But Then I'd Have to Kill You*, and picture books like *Neither* and *Peanut Butter and Cupcake* are great examples of high concept ABA ideas that have been realized in print.

Every editor loves to see great high concept proposals come across his or her desk, but in the CRA, traditional content is often better. Christianity doesn't ebb and flow with culture as compared to the rest of society. Traditional values, ideas, and concepts are still very marketable in the

CRA and have great sales potential. Every year dozens of books on topics like love, grace, prayer, Easter, and Christmas flood the Christian market. The CRA is predictable because the Bible defines the appropriate boundaries for a healthy Christian lifestyle. Christian publishers create products for people who want to grow deeper in their faith and for people who want clean fiction and children's books that express their biblical worldview.

The Christian Rack and Amazon

Before the downfall and bankruptcy of Family Christian Bookstores, the Christian industry had a significant number of traditional brick-and-mortar stores from which they could sell books. But when Family Christian closed all 240 stores, it sent a tidal wave of grief and despair across the CRA. In light of Family Christian's and other independent bookstores' struggles, many CRA publishers moved to a different model of selling books. Some publishers moved to embrace Amazon and created opportunities to sell more of their books online. Kregel, a mid-sized CRA publisher, now sells 60 percent of its books through Amazon. Others embraced Barnes & Noble and have worked to get their books off the Christian or Inspirational racks and out onto the shelves with all of the other mainstream books. Children's and YA publishers in the CRA have had to edit their content to be "Christian-light" to make this maneuver.

At Barnes & Noble stores, Christian books are limited to a single rack or shelf in the children's section, and adult trade books reside on a one- or two-sided shelf on the main floor. These shelves and racks are usually out of the way, and a reader would only purchase books from these locations if they were already looking for the titles there. Christian books have little to no discoverability in Barnes & Noble, which is why CRA publishers are starting to publish titles with themes and content that won't force them to be limited to these "Christian" locations.

The book *I'm Going to Give You a Bear Hug,* published by ZonderKidz, would otherwise be considered an exclusively ABA title if it wasn't for the single use of the word "prayers" near the end of the book. *I'm Going to Give You a Bear Hug* has managed to make the transition off of the Christian rack and into the mainstream children's department. Publishers will continue to find ways to sell their books, but each year brings new challenges and ever-changing strategies.

Similarities

Even with all these significant differences between the CRA and ABA, some distinct similarities exist. Across both markets, 90 percent of children's/YA titles were sold in print form. Sales are up, and nonfiction is growing steadily. Board books have reached a new high, while picture books have struggled to find buyers. Barnes & Noble recently converted some of its picture book shelves to Middle Grade in an effort to hit the rising trend in Middle Grade. At the writing of this book, publishers have stepped back their releases of picture books because sales are down, and production costs are high.

The market for children's and YA authors is better than ever. Sales are at the highest levels they have ever been in the history of publishing. But the industry isn't as homogenous as it once was, and authors must study each market and each publisher with care to ensure they are submitting proposals and manuscripts that are publishable in the current markets.

Chapter 39

Work-for-Hire
Tracie Heskett

Freelance writers often submit proposals to publishers and hope their book idea will be accepted. But for those who are willing to write for the sake of writing, work-for-hire offers a valid option. To enter the work-for-hire market, it helps to have prior experience (writing and/or working with children), as well as writing samples. That experience may be in the form of presenting content, writing print or online articles, or working in any other context that provides opportunities to compose ideas and words in a clean, organized format.

Getting started in the work-for-hire market requires a willingness to take P.R.I.D.E. in your work, especially as a Christian writer. We take pride in our work when we do the following:

Pray about the assignment. This goes hand-in-hand with the next step, Research. Through prayer, previewing, and research, God guides us in His path for our writing. Preview the assignment to make sure you can deliver what the editor requests. Often, the assignment will be part of a larger project; make sure you understand how all the pieces flow together and where your part fits into the whole.

Research as needed. Study the publisher and their website if the company is new to you. Some assignments may require research in the course of completing the assignment, as well, to become more familiar with the subject matter. For example, I've had to do at least a little research on Bible verses or other fact-checking for most of my work-for-hire assignments in the Christian market.

Inquire of the editor(s) as needed. Clarify the assignment by asking questions if you're unclear about how to proceed. Make sure you have the information you need to complete the assignment as directed.

Develop the content. Think about what you already know about the topic. What might your background knowledge bring to the assignment? Make connections between what you are being asked to write and what you've written in the past; allow your experience to inform your current writing. Use resources the publisher provides and/or outside resources as needed.

Excel to the best of your ability. We honor and bring glory to God when we offer Him our best in all areas, whether our audience is fellow Christians who desire to serve God or those in the general market. We practice excellence when we follow publisher guidelines, meet deadlines, and turn in clean copy. Paying attention to such details shows editors we value and respect them as those "in authority" (in this particular area) over us (1 Peter 2:13-17).

A defining characteristic of work-for-hire is just that: we're working for someone else. This means we keep our editors in mind as we write. Editors appreciate writers who follow the suggestions in the above paragraph, as well as graciously accept and complete rewrites. Communicate professionally, clearly, and concisely with editors to establish working relationships that please those we work for and God.

What does work-for-hire look like? In a perfect world, editors email hopeful authors with an assignment. More often, we may need to send out inquiries. To get started, research publishers' websites and create a list of those who publish the type of writing that best fits your skills and experience. Once an assignment is offered and accepted, you should receive a contract that states the terms of this one-time working relationship between you ("author" or "writer") and the publisher ("company") regarding the content ("work") you will create. Work-for-hire authors often "invoice" as a 1099 vendor, which means sending a statement (bill or invoice) to one or more specific persons in the company who processes author payments. In this case (as a 1099 vendor), the company will not withhold taxes from your check; you will be responsible for setting aside enough to cover any self-employment tax indebtedness. This isn't as scary as it sounds; I've set aside roughly 25 percent of my earnings each year for several years, filed Schedule C and self-employment forms (and paid my own social security tax as part of those forms) and have never been audited. The amount I set aside is always more than enough to cover the taxes on what I earn. The extra is like a "tax return"—I'm happy, and the government is satisfied.

Each of the genres discussed in this section has their own characteristics and guidelines. It's important to study and follow each publisher's guidelines regarding deadlines, content, project overview (for example, purpose and audience), project specifics (for example, sensitivity guidelines, grade-appropriate language/vocabulary and reading level, writing process), format, and reference to related and supportive materials (often provided by the publisher).

Content

Even though work-for-hire involves writing to certain specifications (guidelines), it requires the same creativity and originality as freelance writing. Whether an author writes on assignment or offers their own topic/ideas as a proposal, the writing must be innovative and relevant. When considering relevance, bear in mind timeliness; that is, this piece will be published anywhere from six months to two years in the future. Biography and history topics span across time more readily than science or current events topics, for example. Even within the broad genres of fiction and nonfiction, it's wise to steer clear of topics that might become dated.

Our human experience forms the foundation for much of what we read and write; our writing (regardless of genre) will be grounded in reality. Therefore, research often plays a role, even for fiction projects. For example, a story set in winter is more believable if it gets dark at an appropriate time for the story location. It adds to our credibility as authors when we use reputable sites for research. If applicable, I often include a list of sources as a separate document when I send a completed assignment to an editor. Government (.gov) and academic (.edu) sites offer a wealth of information, often directed specifically toward children and the adults (parents, teachers) who work with them. Some organization (.org) and even commercial (.com) sites provide good information as well; although more careful reading is required to discern any bias.

Speaking of bias, many publishers send a copy of their "sensitivity guidelines" to authors as part of their reference materials. Publishers have specific target audiences, and they do not want to offend or alienate any of their potential readers. The apostle Paul reminded his readers to be sensitive to others in similar ways (Colossians 3:10-12). As children's writers, we want to remember to include a balance of genders, ethnic and social groups, and abilities in our stories.

Writing for Different Age Levels

In my experience, publishers' guidelines will often specify the desired reading levels for a project. Content may be "leveled" using one or more programs: Flesch-Kincaid (available within the Spelling & Grammar tab in Word), Lexile (free subscription available for passages of less than a thousand words), and Fountas & Pinnell (F&P). Spend a little time learning how to use each of these systems and identify the reading level(s) when you submit your writing—for work-for-hire and otherwise. Adjust the reading level of a text by checking word choice (number of syllables) and sentence length and complexity and use active voice whenever possible. Print and online resources (for example, the *Children's Writer's Word Book*) provide information about grade appropriate vocabulary.

It's not always easy to find work-for-hire, especially in the Christian market, but it's a valid way to get into writing for children. Writing primarily as a "freelance" author requires an investment of time in marketing and researching publishers. Work-for-hire requires preparation in terms of writing samples and researching publishers to find a good fit, as well as sending out inquiries, similar to sending proposals to agents and editors. The process of sending out inquiries takes patience, as we wait on God to open doors and guide us in His path to *walk* with Him to write for and bless children.

An Editor's Journey

Catherine DeVries
Publisher
Kregel Books

What do you love about publishing CRA children's through YA books?

I love passing along our faith as Christians to the next generation, through excellent, highly engaging content and visuals.

What types of books are you looking to acquire?

Kregel is looking for biblically based concepts that are clever, imaginative, and/or delightful and express truths about God, the Bible, and what a Christian life looks like, whether that be ourselves individually or in community with each other. We are interested in picture books, Bible storybooks, chapter books (early grade and middle grade selectively), devotionals, and other nonfiction. We are not interested in special format, other than board books, at this time.

What advice can you give to up-and-coming CRA authors?

If you have a passion for writing and for children, spend time with them—lots of time. In my graduate child development coursework, I observed preschoolers for thirty minutes at a time. This helped me go beyond my initial impressions into deeper insights, such as story scripting, social interaction, attention span, large motor skills, fine motor skills, verbal expression, and behavioral patterns. It all begins with a love for your audience. Be sure you know them well. Your stories will resonate with them all the more if you put in the time and research, beyond your instincts about what will work and what won't. And also, be sure to TEST your concept on children. They are very honest! You will quickly discover how they feel about it. In my opinion, writing for children is one of the most difficult crafts of a writer. But what purposeful work this is, as we work together to fulfill Deuteronomy 6:4-9.

SECTION 5

Extra Advice

A Writer's Journey
Caroline George

A uthor of *Dearest Josephine* (Thomas Nelson)

Tell us about the experience of getting your first Christian YA book published?

My publishing journey hasn't been conventional. When I was in high school, I self-published two YA science fiction novels. Then, during my senior year of college, my third book was published by a small press based in Canada. I worked for several publishers, received a degree in publishing and public relations, and spent two whole years writing books. Thomas Nelson expressed interest in my YA action comedy in March 2019. The book went to pub board and resulted in a phone call with the TNZ team. After we talked, they asked me to pitch more book ideas. I pitched over ten concepts. During that process, I turned my women's fiction novel concept (now titled *Dearest Josephine*) into a YA book. The team liked it and offered a three-book contract in July. I signed in September. I didn't plan to write in the Christian market, but I'm so grateful God paired me with Thomas Nelson. I love the team and couldn't ask for a better situation.

Chapter 40

Motivation and Reaction
Bryan Davis

Many young adult readers love action. Some enjoy lots of it. Being authors who want to please readers who are accustomed to the often frenetic activity in fantasy and superhero films, we need to put an I'm-in-the-theater-with-the-characters feel in our scenes.

We accomplish this superpowered feat by employing Motivation/Reaction Units (M/R units). These units are cause-and-effect sequences in a story that show a cycle of cause (motivation), then effect (reaction), and the effect becomes the cause for the next effect and so on.

The foundation of this technique is simple—every action, word, or thought that you write for a point-of-view character should have a reasonably clear motivation; that is, readers have a good idea of why the character acted, whether in thought, word, or deed. For an optimum experience, readers are supposed to feel like they're on the screen with the character, even inside the character's skin and sensing what the character senses. Therefore, readers should know why the character does anything at the moment the action occurs. Nothing should be hidden.

First rule of this technique: Motivation precedes reaction. Readers should know the character's reason for any action before reading the action. For example, the following is wrongly stated:

Misty cringed when the dog barked.

"Misty cringed" is the action (or reaction). The dog barking is the motivation for her action. Since the dog barking was the motivation and occurred first, it should be reported first because when readers see "Misty cringed," for a moment they don't know why she cringed. If they are inside her skin, as they should be, they would know why. For one brief moment they are blinded to the reason for her action, and they lose intimacy.

More examples:

Incorrect: He arched his back and cried for mercy as electricity shot through his body, running up and down his spine.

Correct: Electricity shot through his body, running up and down his spine. He arched his back and cried for mercy.

Incorrect: His head cracked on the floor once more as another jolt shook him, and blackness overcame all his senses.

Correct: As another jolt shook him, his head cracked on the floor once more, and blackness overcame all his senses.

When characters react to motivations, their reactions are usually one or more of the following: an involuntary action, a voluntary action, or speech (spoken aloud or thought). Sometimes a character will react in only one

Motivation and Reaction

of these ways, sometimes two, and sometimes all three. Whenever a character reacts in more than one of these ways, the most natural sequential order is as listed. Involuntary action usually precedes voluntary action or speech, and voluntary action usually precedes speech.

For example: The Doberman snarled. Her legs shaking, Misty ducked behind a skinny tree and cried out, "Help me!"

Misty reacted first with shaking legs (involuntary), then by ducking behind a tree (voluntary), then by crying out. This order of reactions doesn't always hold true, but it is the most natural progression, and it will feel right to readers.

When a character is faced with danger, involuntary reactions can include cringing, ducking out of the way, striking with a fist, or even shouting (though often not with words)—anything that a character would do without consciously thinking about it. These are knee-jerk reactions.

Voluntary reactions include hiding in the cellar, loading a gun, searching for an escape route, or anything that requires conscious thought.

And, of course, reactions differ greatly depending on the kind of stimuli that cause them.

For characters who are not the point-of-view character, readers will often not know what motivates them because readers are not inside their skin. Yet, readers should always understand, without exception, why the point-of-view character does anything, even if the reason appears to be foolish or ill-advised (in the readers' minds).

Like dominoes falling in a line, your story should be a long series of M/R units. Every action, whether physical, spoken, or thought, should be a reaction to something that happened in a recent sentence or paragraph, and that reaction transforms into the motivation for the next reaction.

Let's look at an excerpt from my book *Reapers* to illustrate a longer sequence of these M/R units. Comments are in bold.

Molly choked on the pills and coughed them up **(Reaction to family trying to force feed the pills, not shown)**. Her body stiffened, and she let out a moan **(Reaction to not taking the medicine)**. While the three patted her hands and stroked her head in futility **(Reaction to her moan)**, I swallowed hard. Even after more than three years as a Reaper, the sight of a dying child still tore a hole in my heart. **(Reaction to all of the above)**

My cloak vibrated, sending hot prickles across my arms. **(A Reaper's reaction to impending death.)** The end was near. Only one hope remained—the syringe. **(The impending death sparks an idea, which is a reaction.)**

As I reached into my pocket **(Reaction to thinking about the syringe)**, the rusty hinges at the front door squeaked. Everyone froze. Fiona whispered, "I heard no knock." **(Reactions to the door squeaking)**

Notice that each reaction becomes a motivation for the next reaction, thereby setting up linked chains. The links in the chain are the M/R units, and they continue occurring, one after another after another. Everything happens for a reason, and when the units come in an unbroken series, readers feel like they are in the room while events are happening. Readers are never "out of the loop."

Properly writing these units, however, can become obsessive. It's important to remember that clear writing that helps us tell our stories is more important than the motivation-reaction principles.

Look at this example:

He stopped the flashlight beam on a battery lamp, sat on the floor next to it, and turned it on, keeping it at a low level to save power.

In the strictest sense, this example has two out-of-order motivation/reactions.

1. He stopped the flashlight beam because it came across the lamp, but the text reports the stopping before mentioning the lamp. Readers don't know the motivation for stopping until after the action. That's out of order.

2. The reason for keeping the lamp at a low level is to save power. Therefore, to follow the M/R order perfectly, the writer should mention the motivation of saving power before the reaction, that is, keeping the lamp at a low level.

Since the motivations come immediately after the reactions, only a little harm to reader intimacy is likely. If the writer has difficulty figuring out how to alter the order without making the phrasing awkward, then it might be better to leave it alone. In other words, don't obsess over this principle.

Still, if you want to avoid any loss of intimacy, you can probably find a way to rewrite a paragraph to keep the motivation/reaction sequence in the proper order.

Here is one way to do so with the example:

He swept the beam across a battery-powered lamp. "Ah. This will help. No idea how long it's been here, though." He sat on the floor next to the lamp and turned it on at a low level. The dim glow illuminated the cavern, allowing him to flick his penlight off.

Since there is no mention of stopping the beam, that out-of-order phrase is no longer an issue. Also, his mention of wondering how long the lamp's been there implies that he's concerned that it might not work, giving reason for turning it on at a low level, which sets the motivation and reaction in their proper order.

To master this writing tool, I highly recommend reading *Techniques of the Selling Writer* by Dwight V. Swain.

Among other vital issues, he goes into detail about M/R units, concluding with:

> Writers ... will recognize the M-R unit for what it is: a tool, infinitely valuable, whose use they must master so completely that its skilled manipulation becomes automatic and instinctive. ... How do you least painfully achieve such mastery? ... To write in whatever manner comes easiest for you, paying no attention to any rules whatever. Then, go back over your copy and check to make sure that each reaction is motivated; that each motivating stimulus gets a reaction, and that ineptitude in use of language has not in any way confused the issue.

Practice will make this skill seem like second nature. You will begin seeing unmotivated actions as if they were warning lights. A strong motivation that lacks a reaction will seem like a lost orphan begging to be noticed. Broken links in M/R unit chains will appear to be gaping holes that demand transitions.

Also, you will recognize that you have applied this tool correctly when you try to insert something new in an earlier part of your story, such as a foreshadowing element, and you can't find a place to put it because the insertion will break an M/R unit link. Congratulations. Your M/R chain is strong.

Catherine Jones Payne
Catherine Jones Payne is an author of young adult fantasy novels and an editor for small presses and indie authors. Her editing clients have won Carol and Christy awards, landed on the *USA Today* bestseller list, and appeared on *Good Morning America*.

What advice can you give to first-time authors?

Characters need to have weaknesses, and they need to have internal struggles. This becomes especially true at the middle grade and young adult levels. Loving Jesus doesn't mean we have everything figured out, and if our characters have everything figured out because we're trying to write good moral examples for readers, they won't ring true.

Are there any marketing tips you can share to encourage other children's book authors?

Don't discount the homeschool market! I love going to homeschool conferences to sell my books. Homeschoolers tend to be voracious, thoughtful readers, and their parents are often looking for content that's age-appropriate and written by Christians. It's a win-win situation for everyone—I've had homeschool moms hug me because they're so grateful to find edifying books that their kids are really interested in.

Are there any platform-building tips you can share to encourage other children's book authors?

Start building your platform sooner rather than later

and think carefully about who you're selling to. If your books are written for middle-grade audiences or younger, you're marketing to your readers' parents. If you write for the young-adult market, you're more often marketing to the readers themselves. Cultivate your social media presence according to where your target market is. Ten years ago, the teens were on Facebook. Today, they're on Instagram. In five years, they might be somewhere else.

Chapter 41

Find the Heart of Your Story
Michelle Medlock Adams

Whether you're writing nonfiction or fiction, there's one element that turns a good story into a great one—heart. But, just how do you find the heart of a story? It all starts with a little investigative journalism.

I began my writing career as a newspaper journalist, and I learned early on the importance of asking the right questions. To really bring a story to life and find the heart of that story, I had to dig deeper than simply asking and answering the "who, what, when, where, why, and how" questions. Sure, sharing the information gathered by answering those basic questions provided enough for a "just the facts" kind of story, and sometimes, that's enough for a straight news piece. But, as children's writers, we have to be better than that. We have to ask the questions and search for the answers that drive the story.

Sometimes that means homing in on just one of the questions and letting that be the focal point of your story, the driving force, the heart. In my holiday picture book, *Little Colt's Palm Sunday* (Ideals Children's Books), answering the "who" question brought my story to life. Once I answered that, I was able to write this retelling of Palm Sunday in a new and unique way. In my story, the "who" was a little colt whose great-great grandfather carried Mary when she was pregnant with Jesus. As he learns about his great-great grandfather's important job, he longs to do something important too. And, he gets his chance when he's asked to carry Jesus through the streets on Palm Sunday. That "who" element drives the story and leads to the heart, which is woven throughout the text. Without stating it, children learn that even though they are little, they can do big things for God.

In *The Rough Patch* by New York Times best-selling author Brian Lies, the "what" in this beautiful and powerful story is loss and grief, but the author didn't stop with the "what." He continued exploring the path that loss often takes when one is grieving, and that eventually ended in hope. Had the author stopped at loss, he would have robbed us of facing anger head-on and finally allowing ourselves to hope again.

Every time I read *The Rough Patch*, tears fill my eyes as I turn the final page of this perfect picture book. In case you haven't read it, let me share the highlights. We encounter a fox named Evan and his dog. They are best friends. They do most everything together, and they especially love working in Evan's gorgeous garden until the unthinkable happens. After his precious dog passes, Evan buries him in the corner of the garden, and nothing is the same again.

Over the next few spreads, we see Evan go from sad to mad. He takes a hoe and chops down his garden, allowing the weeds to take over. The prickly garden matches his mood. You can literally feel the hopelessness and anger emanating from the pages.

Thankfully, the author doesn't leave us there. Despite Evan's neglect, a large pumpkin grows in his garden—so big that he enters it in the county fair and wins third place. The prize? Ten dollars or a puppy. At first, Evan says he will take the ten dollars but then decides it wouldn't hurt to just look inside the box. The last spread shows Evan driving away from the fair with his new pup sitting next to him in his truck.

The author takes readers through the stages of grief, but he doesn't do it by explaining what those stages are and how we can get through them. Instead, he shows Evan feeling sad and lonely, shutting himself off from the world. And then we experience his "new normal" as he deals with life without his best friend. He's mad. He's hurt. But eventually, he allows himself to let his guard down and possibly love again. When the book ends, he's hopeful. And, so are we, his grateful readers.

The *Rough Patch* is one of my favorite books because it is brilliantly written and because it has such heart.

Another great way to find the heart of a story is to find a story with heart. In other words, look for a story that has a little-known fact or an interesting detail that evokes emotion. My friend Nancy Churnin does this so well. She's the author of award-winning books such as *Manjhi Moves a Mountain* about a man who moved a mountain one bucket at a time to help the people of his village, and *William Hoy*—the story of a deaf baseball player who forever changed America's favorite pastime.

"I found myself particularly drawn to people who aren't the biggest or strongest, but who have the heart to persevere against the odds," Churnin said in an interview she gave to fellow nonfiction ninja Stephanie Bearce. "The minute I learned about this man who spent 22 years chiseling a path through a 300-foot mountain so that the kids in his poor village could get to school and the sick could get to a doctor on the other side, I knew I had to write his story." (https://fabulateacher.wordpress.com/2019/04/04/meet-author-nancy-churnin/)

As Churnin has shown, some nonfiction stories already have the heart element just waiting for you to discover and share in such a way that children all over the world will be challenged and changed.

If you'll ask the right questions and never settle for the easy answers, and if you'll spend time researching those little-known stories that need to be told as well as those hidden facts about well-known events or people, you'll run smackdab into the heart of the story.

Chapter 42

Contests
Cyle Young

One of the ways a writer can get noticed by industry professionals is through winning writing contests. Publishers and agents often look for authors who can write well enough to stand out above their peers.

Contests can help speed up an agent's or publisher's search process, as it allows an industry professional to circumvent the slush pile and look at the strongest manuscripts. Contests can help separate the wheat from the chaff. Award recognition is a potentially healthy sign of writing ability.

If you aren't entering writing contests, you need to be. Contests can help your writing career in various ways.

1. *Contests require you to meet deadlines.*
   Any writer, worth their salt, is capable of meeting a publisher or agent's deadline. Contest deadlines

push you to write well in a tight timeframe.
2. *Contests build your writing resume.*
   Winning awards helps you pad your writing bio. This is essential early in your writing career, as most beginning writers don't have a lot of published work to include in their author bio.
3. *Contests help you find an agent or publisher.*
   Many agents and publishers serve as judges in contests. It gives them opportunities to discover new talent, find new clients, and see how your work stacks up against similar competition. Christian writer's conferences often have contests that allow your work to get noticed by the industry professionals who are on faculty at those events.
4. *Contests stretch your writing ability.*
   Competition drives us to improve. When you know your work will be judged against others, you strive to create your best manuscript, applying learned skills, and strengthening your writing.
5. *Contests allow you to gain perspective.*
   Sometimes we need a reality check. You may think your manuscript is amazing, but in reality, it needs some work. Many contests offer constructive feedback, which can give you critical insight into improving your writing.
6. *Contests help you get published.*
   Many contests offer publishing opportunities to winners and/or finalists. If you enter these contests and win, you may also find yourself published in a magazine or anthology. Or better yet, you may land that all-important book contract.

Writing contests are an important and necessary part of the writing lifestyle. Take time to search for contests that have deadlines within the next few months and begin writing and editing. Don't wait for your writing to be perfect before you enter. Winning a contest may help you get one step closer to publishing your first or next Christian children's book.

Chapter 43

Contracts
Cyle Young

Every author longs to sign a first or next book contract. But not all contracts are equal, and the publisher is never in the business of ensuring all your rights are protected. Publishing is a business, and publishers desire to make money. To do that, they need to acquire a book with favorable terms that ensures the publishing house sells enough books to recoup expenses and carve out a nice profit.

Christian publishers are also businesses, and the publishing contracts crafted by their attorneys are never weighted in your favor. At traditional publishers, a contract liaison or attorney will negotiate the terms of your contract, not the acquisition editor, who has championed your book. As much as you want to believe a Christian publisher would give you the best deal, that is counterintuitive to running a successful publishing business. As an author, it is ALWAYS wise to have an agent or attorney advise you or assist you in negotiating better terms in your publishing contract.

Some areas of the contract terms you need to be aware of:

1. **Description of the Work**
    a. This portion of the contract describes the work being contracted. This section needs to be accurate to the work being contracted and specify the estimated word count.

2. **Grant of Rights**
    a. This section describes which rights you are contracting to the publisher. It also covers the media and languages in which the publisher can publish your book.
    b. The rights you generally grant the publisher refer to just the physical printing of the book in paperback and hardcover. They also give the publisher the right to print, manufacture, and distribute your work.

3. **Advance and Payment Schedule**
    a. An advance payment is an advance against royalties.
    b. Not every contract comes with an advance, but those that do should clearly state how much advance is being paid and in how many payments it will be apportioned. It's also important to know what is required of you as an author to receive each payment.

4. **Royalties and Payment Schedule**
    a. Royalties are only received after the publisher

has recouped the entirety of the advance.
   b. This section of the contract should state what percentage of the profits or retail purchase price goes to the author. Most Christian publishers offer royalties off of the net profits and not off of the retail price. Because of this, the percentages with some publishers may be higher than their counterparts in the general market, who base royalty percentages off of the retail price.
   c. Royalties can be paid monthly, quarterly, bi-annually, or annually.

5. **Subsidiary Rights**
   a. Sub-rights, as they are often called, are rights granted to subsidiary organizations who will publish or create books, products, or media based off the property contracted. These rights bring in additional revenue streams for the publisher and author. This section should clearly state what percentage of the subsidiary income goes to the author and the publisher.
   b. Sample rights are mass market paperback, foreign languages, audio, TV, film, merchandising, serial rights, and more. Make sure you know what rights the publisher is acquiring and don't give any away that you initially wanted to retain.

6. **Option and Non-Compete Clause**
   a. Most publishers' default contracts include an option clause. An option gives the publisher the first option or exclusive option on your next project. An option clause is not always the right situation for every book, and you should never sign an option that forces you to accept

predetermined deal terms on your next book.
   b. Every contract includes a non-competition clause. Publishers want to sell your book; they don't want to compete against similar books in the market, especially those written by you. Your contract will restrict you against competing against your own book, but they can also pigeonhole your future publishing options. Make sure your competition clause is not any broader than it needs to be.

7. **Author's Rights**
   a. An author needs to understand their rights for sharing portions of the book on the blog or website or in marketing. Most contracts clearly communicate which permissions an author has, and those permissions are generally more limited than most authors anticipate if they haven't negotiated a contract before.

8. **Reversion of Rights**
   a. It's always wonderful to sign a book contract, but you also need to ensure that you know how to get out of the contract if the relationship with the publisher goes sour.
   b. This section will describe how you get your rights back at the end of the contract term, due to a publisher's bankruptcy, if there are unresolvable issues with your publisher, or if your book has low sales.

Chapter 44

Agents in the Christian Market
Cyle Young

An agent is not required in the Christian market. An author can still sell a book directly to a publisher, but with each passing quarter, it is getting progressively more difficult to get published in the Christian market without literary agency representation. This change is directly related to publishers' increasing reliance on an author's platform and marketing help.

As an author myself, I believe an agent is necessary. Every author should attempt to work with a literary agent. Even a bad literary agent can be better than working on your own. Lawyers are not an adequate substitute unless, by some chance, they work in the publishing industry every day—that is extremely rare, and when you find one, generally more expensive than having an agent.

Agents charge a 15 percent commission for their services, and they only get paid when they assist you with selling or negotiating your work. A good agent will provide much more value than the 15 percent advance and royalties you sacrifice to work with them. Agents negotiate better terms, help you get more money, and they protect your interests and rights. They also provide a wealth of industry knowledge, advice, and encouragement. Publishers and their attorneys are not in the interest of protecting your rights. Remember, this is business—agents help you treat it as a business, and they equip you to make the best business decision for your book and career.

The easiest way to get any agent is to already have a book deal in hand—yes, it is still wise to get an agent before you negotiate and sign the contract. I've seen too many authors saddle themselves and their career by signing contracts without representation. Don't make this mistake.

You pitch an agent just like you pitch a publisher. You can meet them in person or submit to them via their website or email. Make sure you follow the agent's guidelines and always send them your best, well-edited work.

Chapter 45

Ghostwriting and Adapting Books
Tama Fortner

You may have seen it—that name spelled out in tiny letters on the cover of a favorite book. It's sometimes accompanied by a "with" or an "adapted by." And it's often tucked under the larger, sixty-four-point type of a more famous author's name. Who is that person in the tiny type? That's the ghostwriter—or adapter, as the case may be.

Ghostwriting and Adaptations: What Are They? And What's the Difference?

Ghostwriting

Ghostwriting usually involves writing a manuscript from scratch. A publisher may approach a ghostwriter with a particular idea or concept in mind, but it is up to the ghostwriter to put that idea or concept into words. You might be doing research and interviews with the named "author," or the work may be entirely of your own creation. The result may be a stand-alone work, the continuation of a series, or something that will fit into an established author's line of books.

Adaptation

An *adaptation*—in the context of children's writing—is taking a work created for adults and rewriting, or *adapting*, it for a younger audience. That audience might be teen, middle grade, elementary, or even younger. Depending on the audience, only a few changes to the original work may be needed here and there. Or it may require a complete overhaul.

Who Gets the Credit?

For both ghostwriting and adaptations, the "credit" for the work varies from project to project. Your name may appear on the cover, title page, or copyright page—or not at all. Obviously, getting your name on the book is helpful for building your reputation as a writer; however, even "anonymous" works will help you establish relationships with editors.

Check Your Ego

When writing as a ghostwriter or adapting a work for someone else, it's not about you. You may disagree with word choice, style, or presentation, but this is the time to bow to your editor's wishes. Review projects carefully before accepting. If you disagree with an author or publisher on a theological or other issue important to you, this is not the time to assert your own opinions. Simply pass on the project and find another one.

A Different Kind of Writing

When working through an adaptation or a ghostwriting project for children, there are a few things to keep in mind

Find Your Voice ... and Lose It
As writers, we are encouraged to find our own writing voice. But when it comes to adaptations and ghostwriting, you need to lose your voice and, instead, mimic the author (or line of books) you're writing for. How? *Read and listen.* Read the author's books, blog posts, and interviews. Listen to the podcasts and videos. What patterns do you notice? Is this author fond of alliteration or repetition? Is any humor used? What types of examples are used? Work to incorporate the key elements of that author's voice and style into your manuscript.

Make It Relevant
Books for adults are, of course, written for adults. The illustrations and examples they use may not be meaningful to younger readers. As you're working through an adaptation, be sure to replace any grownup illustrations with ones your target age group will relate to. For example, kids aren't going to relate to the stress of life at the office, but every school-age child knows the stress of walking into a lunchroom and searching for a welcoming face and a place to sit.

Include the issues kids today struggle with—they might surprise you. Issues that we once reserved for the teen or even young adult years are now popping up in younger and younger age groups. Things like anxiety, perfectionism, body image, stress, and time management. Search the internet for journal articles related to things like "children's fears," "children's stress," or "things children worry about."

Make It Real
While abstract and figurative language can make perfect sense to a grownup, whenever possible, use more concrete examples when adapting or ghostwriting a work for kids. For example, instead of writing about a jellyfish with a body ten inches in diameter, write about a jellyfish with a body *as big as a basketball!*

Watch Your Words
We may know what words like "transformation" and "resurrection" mean, but be ready to explain them to younger audiences. Know when children learn certain words and concepts. An internet search for word lists by grade level, or a book such as the *Children's Writer's Word Book*, can be most helpful when you're trying to choose just the right word.

Know Your Audience
If you want to write for kids, you need to know kids. Read what they're reading, listen to what they listen to, and watch what they watch. Try your hand at a video game or two. And above all, hang out with them. Volunteer at your church, observe at a school or library, or be a volunteer tutor. Serve while you learn!

Message over Me
I once had someone tell me that she would *never* be a ghostwriter or do work-for-hire projects. She felt it was a betrayal to her writing to work anonymously or to sign over rights and royalties. While I understand her stance, it can be limiting in today's marketplace. Would I mind seeing my own name in sixty-four-point type on a cover?

Of course not! But as a now best-selling ghostwriter and adapter, if I had insisted on author credit and royalties from the beginning, I would have missed literally *millions* of opportunities to tell the world about Jesus. And isn't that what this is truly about?

Pray Always

As writers for children—*Christian* writers for children—we are blessed with the opportunity to share the truth of Jesus with untold numbers of little ones. With that privilege comes an even greater responsibility. As you sit down to write, ponder your words. Pray over them. Hold them up to His light for inspection—and make sure your words are a reflection of His Word.

Chapter 46

The Research Trail
Wendy Hinote Lanier

Writing for the nonfiction children's market is a lot of fun. Better still, nonfiction is a hot commodity in both the general and the Christian children's book markets. As its popularity grows, so does the demand.

Good nonfiction always begins with a solid base of research. Many people find that a bit scary. But it needn't be. Research is merely finding answers to questions about a given topic. All you have to do is find the answers from a reliable source.

Some Helpful and Reliable Sources

If you're new to nonfiction writing, you may not yet have a feel for what is a reliable source. Some great starting places are websites connected to government archives that can provide reliable historical and scientific information. Some websites you may find helpful are:

- Smithsonian – www.si.edu where you'll find links for students, educators, and researchers. A search of the Smithsonian site will give you an idea about whether they have any information that pertains to your topic.
- The National Archives – www.archives.gov preserves and protects official documents about our nation and our way of life. The site provides access to the essential documentation of the rights of American citizens and the actions of their Government.
- The Library of Congress – www.loc.gov has one of the largest collections of books, maps, films, newspapers, periodicals, etc. in the world. The search feature makes it easy to find what you're looking for. Just be prepared. There might be more than you ever imagined. You may have to narrow the parameters of your search to find a more manageable amount of material.
- The American Museum of Natural History – www.amnh.org is also a good source of information. Enter your subject in the search bar to see how many articles pertain to your topic.
- When you need a professional quote or the latest information on a topic, try ProfNet.com. It's free for writers and journalists. The site can help you make a connection with an expert who can help you make sure your information is correct and up to date.
- Help a Reporter Out (www.helpareporter.com) is another site that pairs experts and writers. You do have to sign up for this one, and there may be a fee. It depends on your level of access.
- Newspapers.com is an online newspaper archive run by Ancestry.com. It has over three hundred years of newspapers from towns all over the world.

There is a fee, and the price depends on the level of access you desire.
- ➢ WorldCAT and JSTOR are both databases. Access can usually be gotten through your local library. Both are a bit intimidating for novice researchers, but your local librarian can help guide you in finding what you need there.

Christian authors working on pieces for the CRA market may find Biblegateway.com and Sermons.com helpful. Biblegateway.com is an online Bible reference tool for finding scriptures in various versions of the Bible. It's free, but there is a for-pay version that has fewer ads and more in-depth Bible study aids. The site also includes a blog and articles on a variety of topics. Sermons.com has three levels of yearly subscriptions. They provide ideas and content for children's and adult sermons. The topics and scripture references can be helpful if you're writing along a particular theme.

Additional Tools and Tips

When writing a nonfiction manuscript there is, invariably, some type of measurement involved. Depending on the topic, you will likely be including a numerical size, weight, or distance. Educational publishers will generally ask you to provide metric conversions to show both standard and metric measurements. Years ago, I chanced across a conversion website I still use. World Wide Metric is a company that sells valves, flanges, and gaskets. But their website also includes a conversion chart that lets you fill in your measurement and get metric and standard equivalents. The chart is found at http://www.worldwidemetric.com/measurements.html. You can also use https://www.metric-conversions.org/. Both of these calculators take all the guesswork out of making the conversion for you.

To help keep track of all your research, I suggest bookmarking articles and information as you go. You can take that a step further and either make a hard copy of the article, or copy and paste it into a document on your computer. I keep folders of the information for a particular project both on my computer and in my files. That's overkill, I know. But it works for me. Probably only one of those is a good idea for you.

It's also a good idea to purge your bookmarks after you've completed your project. Otherwise, your list just keeps growing. After a while, it can get unwieldy.

And finally, one of the best things you can do for yourself is to make friends with your local research librarian. If you are an alumnus of a university, take advantage of their library resources and the expertise of their research librarians. There is also usually someone at your local public library who is well versed in research sources. They can be invaluable in helping you narrow down the field of information you find to something you can really use. Sometimes they'll even offer to do some of the work for you because they enjoy the hunt. They can show you how to use their databases (including ones like WorldCAT and JSTOR) and help you track down and order whatever you need.

This is, by no means, a definitive list of research tools. Thanks to the internet, the world is literally at your fingertips. The key is to understand that all sources are not created equal. Maybe you've heard the old adage, "Consider the source." That's especially true of nonfiction research. Make sure your source is credible. And don't let the thought of having to do research keep you from tackling a nonfiction project. If the topic interests you, go for it!

Chapter 47

Diversity
Edwina Perkins

Where Do We Begin?

As a child, I learned a very popular children's song that addressed a love for all the children in the world. Four skin tones were mentioned in the melody, yet the ethnicities of today reach far beyond red, yellow, black, and white.

As our nation continues to grow in ethnic diversity, so do our children. Statistics show that in the classrooms of 2020, 50 percent of children ages ten and under come from multi-ethnic families. (Children's Book Summit, Nielsen Bookscan). Yet, according to Diversity in Children's Books 2018, less than 25 percent of children's books depict characters from a diverse background compared to the depiction of 27 percent of animals/others and 50 percent of whites.

This large imbalance in representation can be attributed to the fact that children's literature is overwhelmingly written by white authors. The publishing industry as well is mainly a white industry.

There has been an increase in the number of African American characters in children's books from six percent in 2008 to eleven percent in 2019, but proportionally this is a small improvement. Ashley Finley in the article, *Where Is the Black Blueberries for Sal?* states, "Writers often follow the common advice to 'write what they know,' and gatekeepers tend to greenlight projects that tell stories about people like themselves." (https://www.theatlantic.com/family/archive/2019/05/the-lack-of-diversity-in-childrens-books-about-nature/590152/)

What Is Diversity?

Diversity means having a range of differences. I would add when it comes to diversity with people and culture, there needs to be an understanding that each ethnic group or individual is unique and different. Those differences aren't meant to divide but to broaden another's perspective on a life outside of his own. Diversity in society can create cultural sensitivity and insight as well as help to build bridges and understanding across cultures.

Why Diversity in Books Is Important

All children need to be able to see themselves in the books they read. It allows them to see they are not alone and shows them that their world is important. When children see themselves, they gain a sense that their world has value. Not only do children need to see diversity in books, but they need to see the characters in prominent roles.

Books are a safe place for children to learn and ask questions. Diverse books teach them about others and help promote empathy and respect. For every child who can see their world in a book, many more are introduced to a world outside of their own.

Diversity

"Most adults in the U.S. spend their formative years in elementary school classrooms. It is their introduction to community outside the family and to the world. It is the breeding ground for much of the empathy and enmity we carry around as adults."[1]

The power of words can change lives. Books can encourage, enlighten, and create compassion. Diversity in books has the power to build bridges where misunderstanding of differences creates division. Children's books can be mirrors or windows to other worlds and allow a child to walk in the shoes of another's experiences.

If a children's song written so long ago can embrace the differences in *all* the children of the world, it's time our society tries to do the same.

Resources for Children's Books on Diversity (and Some Good Reads for Adults Too!)

Here are just a few places to search for books on diversity, but use wisdom with your search.

> http://hereweeread.com/2018/11/the-2019-ultimate-list-of-diverse-childrens-books.html
> https://diversebooks.org/resources/where-to-find-diverse-books/
> https://www.thebump.com/a/childrens-books-about-diversity
> https://www.nytimes.com/interactive/2016/09/22/books/23racebooks.html

---

[1] Jennie McDonald, "Diversity in Children's Literature: Check Your Blind Spot, Part 2," Collaborative Classroom, https://www.collaborativeclassroom.org/blog/diversity-in-childrens-literature-check-your-blind-spot-part-2/.

Conclusion
Cyle Young

As you have seen throughout this book, writing and selling Christian children's books is not as easy as it may first seem. Yes, these books are targeted for young children and teens 0-18, but their content, formatting, and themes vary greatly by age level, religious beliefs, and denominational affiliation. And even though the juvenile Christian market resembles the more grandiose general market (ABA), the nuances and uniqueness of the Christian market add layers of complexity that can take weeks, months, even years to effectively navigate.

The Christian market allows authors to write with a greater purpose. To share the light of Jesus Christ with the world through board books, picture books, chapter books, middle-grade books, and all the way up to Young Adult novels. That call is unique to Christian authors, we who choose to share our faith in a more overt manner, and also to those of us who want to write from a Christian worldview, but in such a way that won't alienate secular readers.

We hope you'll study these chapters and apply the writing insights to your own stories. Write God's answer for a lost and broken world and challenge your readers to live their lives to the fullest. Let God use you and let your words speak boldly to each and every child, teen, and adult who are blessed to discover them.

Michelle and I are excited to be part of your journey, and we look forward to seeing your articles and books in print!

Contributor Biographies

Michelle Medlock Adams is an award-winning writer of over one hundred books, including her latest for children, *Cuddle-Up Prayers* and *I Love You Bigger Than the Sky*. She has earned more than seventy industry accolades, such as her first-place honors from the Associated Press, the Society of Professional Journalists, the Golden Scrolls, the Selahs, the Moonbeam Children's Book Awards, and the Illumination Awards, to name a few. She is also a NY Times best-selling ghostwriter and a best-selling children's author with close to four million books sold.

She is married to her high school sweetheart, Jeff, and they have two grown daughters, two sons-in-law, two grandsons, and two granddaughters. When not writing, teaching writing, or speaking at women's events, Michelle enjoys bass fishing, Doris Day movies, cheering on the Chicago Cubbies, and all things leopard print. You can learn more about her at www.michellemedlockadams.com and by following her @INwritergirl on Twitter, Instagram, and Pinterest.

Shannon Anderson is a teacher, presenter, and children's book author. She was named one of the Top 10 Teachers who inspired "The Today Show" in 2019. She served as the regional advisor for the Indiana SCBWI and has authored ten books for children and two books for teachers. You can learn more at: www.shannonisteaching.com.

Steve Bootsma is a former teacher, corporate trainer, and now executive director of a Christian non-profit boy's club ministry. He has been investing in the lives of children for over thirty years.

Crystal Bowman is an award-winning, best-selling author of more than one hundred books for children including *Does God Take Naps?* and *M Is for Manger*. She also writes lyrics for children's piano music and stories for *Clubhouse Jr Magazine*. She and her husband have three grown children and seven huggable grandchildren. www.crystalbowman.com.

Rev. Dr. Robin Currie learned story sharing reading Jesus' parables and sitting on the floor for children's sermons and library storytimes. Her interactive books include the *Baby Bible Storybook* series and *The Very Best Story Ever Told: the Gospel with American Sign Language*. She writes stories to read and read again!

Bryan Davis is the author of the following young adult fantasy series: Dragons in our Midst, Oracles of Fire, Children of the Bard, The Reapers Trilogy, Echoes from the Edge, and Dragons of Starlight. He also wrote *I know Why the Angels dance*, a contemporary novel for adults. Bryan's novels have been readily accepted in schools worldwide, whether public, Christian (Protestant or Catholic), Jewish, or otherwise. Such is their wide appeal. For more information, see his website—www.daviscrossing.com.

Contributor Biographies

A multi-passionate creative fueled mostly by coffee, **Victoria Duerstock** relentlessly pursues her dreams. Writing, speaking, and helping creatives grow their platforms with DIY and done-for-you solutions keeps her busy! Her first children's title is *Christmas Crafts and Advent Devotions for Kids* (Skyhorse). Read more at www.victoriaduerstock.com.

Catherine DeVries is Publisher of Kregel Publications, with nearly thirty years of experience in Christian publishing and a proven track record of crafting best-selling Bibles, books, and ministry resources for all ages. She began her career with Zondervan/HarperCollins, where she helped launch the NIrV translation and Zonderkidz, and acquired The Jesus Storybook Bible. As brand manager at United Methodist Publishing House, DeVries launched the Common English Bible translation. Then as Publisher for David C Cook, Catherine was responsible for Sunday school curriculum lines, trade books, and ministry resources. Catherine is also the author of twenty-five children's books.

Tama Fortner is a best-selling writer with more than thirty titles to her credit. She is also the ghostwriter behind some of the CRA's best-selling titles for children. Follow her on Facebook and Instagram, and find out more at her website: www.TamaFortner.com

Caroline George is a multi-award-winning author of YA fiction. (Her book *Dearest Josephine* releases from Thomas Nelson, Harper Collins in 2021.) She graduated from Belmont University with a degree in publishing and public relations and now travels the country, speaking at conferences and writing full-time. Find her on Instagram @authorcarolinegeorge.

Deb Haggerty is the Publisher and Editor-in-Chief for Elk Lake Publishing Inc. Elk Lake "publishes the positive" consisting primarily of fiction for all genres and age groups from children's to adult. Nonfiction submissions must have a twist—be out of the ordinary.

Tessa Emily Hall is an award-winning author for teens. Her passion for shedding light on clean entertainment for youth led her to a career as a Literary Agent at Cyle Young Literary Elite, YA Acquisitions Editor for Illuminate YA (LPC Imprint), and Founder/Editor of PursueMagazine.net. Learn more about her at www.TessaEmilyHall.com.

P. K. Hallinan has written and illustrated more than one hundred children's books. He is an ordained minister and an accomplished musician. P. K. lives with his wife, Jeanne, and their dog, Sadie, in Talent, Oregon.

Tracie Heskett is a best-selling author whose work-for-hire contracts include fiction and nonfiction leveled readers and reading passages for grades 1-12. She has also written over fifty teacher resource books, a textbook, and other curriculum materials for national Christian and secular educational publishers. Tracie has also ghostwritten two books and a workbook.

Amy Houts is the author of over seventy books for young children including, *God's Protection Covers Me* (Beaming Books). It's a joy for Amy to share Bible truths and God's love with young children through her writing. Amy and her husband, Steve, are the parents of two grown daughters and have three grandchildren.

Steven James is an award-winning storyteller and the critically acclaimed author of more than fifty books. He has been writing and telling stories to children since 1989.

Bethany Jett is a former youth minister's wife and high school cheerleading coach whose first book was a dating guide for young women. She is a military wife to her college sweetheart, business owner, and momma-of-boys who loves planners, suspense novels, cute shoes, and all things girly. Connect with Bethany at BethanyJett.com.

Wendy Hinote Lanier is a former elementary teacher and a Texan through and through. She writes and speaks for children and adults on a variety of topics. She is the author of more than forty books for children and young adults on topics related to science, technology, social studies, the arts, and, of course, Texas.

Nancy Lohr is Acquisitions Editor at JourneyForth Books. She has been a teacher and school librarian and has worked in publishing for twenty-five years, acquiring and editing manuscripts. She has written two youth novels, curriculum stories and articles, and numerous book reviews and articles for parents and teachers.

Jill Roman Lord is a mother of three grown children. She loved reading books to her kids and enjoyed the years when her kids read to her. She has been married to Bill for over thirty years. They enjoy traveling, running, and visiting their children wherever they may be.

Dandi Daley Mackall is an award-winning author of over five hundred books, from ages 0-adult, *Larger-Than-Life Lara, Winnie the Horse Gentler, My First Book of Psalms; Flipside Books,* and so many more. The recipient of many writing accolades, Dandi was recently awarded the Helen Keating Ott Award for Lifetime Contributions to Children's

Literature. She writes from rural Ohio, where she lives with her family, including horses, dogs, cats, fish, degus, tortoise, and an occasional squirrel, deer, or raccoon. www.dandibooks.com, https://www.facebook.com/dandi.mackall.

Christopher P. N. Maselli has written more than fifty books. He is an Evangelical Press Association award-winning children's author of novels, comics, solve-it-yourself mysteries, and more. He holds an MFA in Writing, and on the training portion of WritingMomentum.com, he helps put other children's writers on the fast track to success.

Mary Morgan is a pastor's wife, church secretary, children's worker, and part-time youth leader (and – oh yes, a grandma!). She calls Lansing, MI, her home but has a passion for traveling. She and her family have visited more than twenty-five National Parks, exploring and photographing each one. She shares America's best idea with children through facts and mysterious adventures, hoping to create in them a desire to explore the parks for themselves.

Catherine Jones Payne is a Seattle native who loves the written word, international travel, crashing waves, and good coffee. Her earliest memory involves pulling up a rolling chair to her parents' old DOS computer—while wearing a tiara, naturally—and tapping out a story of kidnapped princesses. By day, she's the executive editor of Quill Pen Editorial and the author of the *Broken Tides* series. She lives in Greenville, SC, with her historian husband, Brendan, and their cats, Mildred and Minerva.

Rachel Pellegrino is the publisher of Little Lamb Books, a traditional children's publisher of elementary, middle grade, and young adult faith-based fiction and non-fiction. Launched in 2015, Little Lamb Books has produced more than a half-dozen award-winning titles that are beautifully illustrated and full of positive, faith-centered messages. Visit www.littlelambbooks.com to learn more.

Edwina Perkins is an award-winning writer, experienced teacher, speaker, and freelance editor. She serves on the Word Weavers International Advisory Committee. She worked as a content editor with Lighthouse Publishing of the Carolinas and now serves as managing editor of Harambee Press—an imprint that seeks to publish ethnic writers and story—with Iron Stream Media. Edwina is also a contributing writer to *Guideposts* magazine.

Doug Peterson is the award-winning author of seventy books, including four historical novels—*The Disappearing Man, The Puzzle People, The Vanishing Woman,* and *The Lincoln League*. He has also authored forty-two books in the popular VeggieTales series. In addition, he has cowritten several books, including *Of Moose and Men* and *The Call of the Mild* with Torry Martin.

Nancy I. Sanders is the award-winning children's author of more than one hundred books. She has coauthored titles for the best-selling Christian historical fiction series, the Imagination Station with Focus on the Family. Nancy has also written two how-to books, *Yes! You Can Learn How to Write Children's Books, Get Them Published, and Build a Successful Writing Career*, along with *Yes! You Can Learn How to Write Beginning Readers and Chapter Books*. www.nancyisanders.com.

Lori Z. Scott writes children's fiction because she's like an atom. She makes everything up. She also has two quirky habits: chronic doodling and lame joke-telling. Neither one impresses her boss, but they still somehow inspired Lori to write a best-selling book series and over one hundred fifty other publications.

Tim Shoemaker is the author of sixteen books. He's written for Focus on the Family *Clubhouse* magazine for fifteen years. He's worked with youth for over twenty-five years—and still loves it. His book, *Code of Silence,* was included in the Booklist Online "Top Ten Crime Novels for Youth."

Janet Surette is an author and Bible teacher. She writes for women at janetsurette.com and is a contributing writer and speaker for The Gospel Coalition Canada in matters of Christian Living and Motherhood. She recently debuted in the CRA with *Scarlett's Spectacles* by B&H Publishing.

Karissa Taylor is an editor at HarperCollins Christian Publishing and has managed and edited some amazing books from Max Lucado, Kathie Lee Gifford, Sadie Robertson, Louie Giglio, Bob Goff, Emily Ley, Sally Clarkson, and many more! She lives in Nashville, Tennessee, with her husband, John, and her two pretty kitties, Zailee and Brownie.

Cyle Young is a former University of Michigan football player and current alumnus. He played defensive line for four years and was part of the university's 1997 National Championship Football Team. During the final two years of his collegiate career, he also participated on the wrestling team.

He is a lead pastor of a church in Michigan and is still married to his college sweetheart, who has blessed him with three wonderful children. Cyle is also a respected literary agent. He has sold more than three hundred of his clients' books to publishing houses and currently represents authors who have combined sales of more than twenty-seven million books.

As an accomplished children's and nonfiction writer in his own right, Cyle has won more than twenty writing awards. Quarry Press will be releasing two of Cyle's own books, *Michigan Motivations: A Year of Inspiration with the University of Michigan Wolverines* and *The Buckeye Candy: Ohio's Trademark Dessert,* while Crosslink Publishing will be releasing Cyle's Bible picture book series.

You can find out more about Cyle at his website www.cyleyoung.com.

Printed in the United States
By Bookmasters